Clement Mansfield Ingleby

Shakespeare's Bones

Clement Mansfield Ingleby

Shakespeare's Bones

ISBN/EAN: 9783744677837

Printed in Europe, USA, Canada, Australia, Japan

Cover: Foto ©Thomas Meinert / pixelio.de

More available books at **www.hansebooks.com**

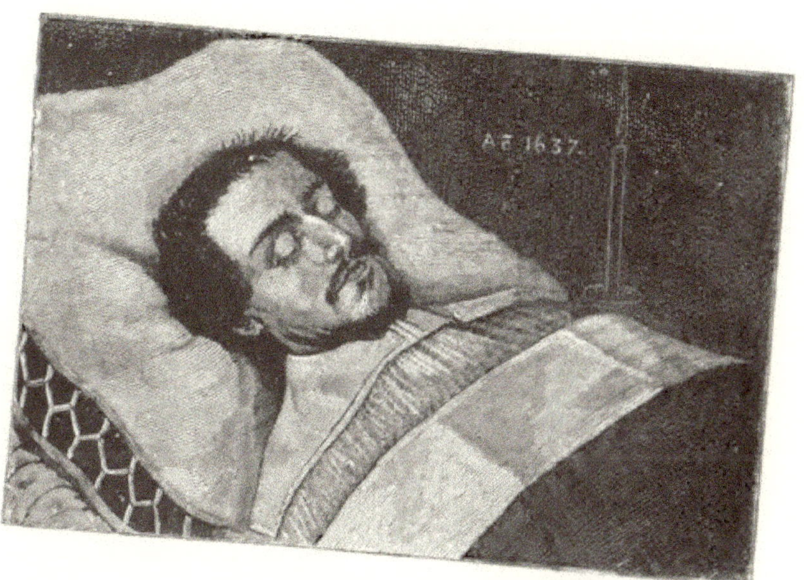
Aº 1637.

Shakespeare's Bones.

THE PROPOSAL TO DISINTER THEM,

CONSIDERED IN RELATION TO THEIR POSSIBLE BEARING ON HIS PORTRAITURE:

ILLUSTRATED BY INSTANCES OF

VISITS OF THE LIVING TO THE DEAD.

BY

C. M. INGLEBY, LL.D., V.P.R.S.L.,

Honorary Member of the German Shakespeare Society,
and a Life-Trustee of Shakespeare's Birthplace, Museum, and New Place,
at Stratford-upon-Avon.

LONDON:

Trübner & Co., 57 & 59, *Ludgate Hill.*

1883.

"Let's talk of graves, of worms, and epitaphs."

Richard II, a. iii, s. 2.

This Essay

IS RESPECTFULLY INSCRIBED

TO

THE MAYOR AND CORPORATION OF STRATFORD-UPON-AVON,

AND THE VICAR

OF THE CHURCH OF THE HOLY TRINITY THERE,

BY THEIR FRIEND AND COLLEAGUE,

THE AUTHOR.

INDEX TO BIBLIOGRAPHY.

SHAKESPEARE'S BONES.

THE sentiment which affects survivors in the disposition of their dead, and which is, in one regard, a superstition, is, in another, a creditable outcome of our common humanity: namely, the desire to honour the memory of departed

CORRIGENDA.

Page.	Line.	Error.	Correction.
1	11	its	our.
2	footnote	Chalfort	Chalfont.
3	10	present	prevent.
22	7	though	through.
36	20	at Sherburn Castle, Dorset	*dele.*
37	6	latter	later one.
38	5 from foot	not	*dele.*
44	2 ,, ,,	gentlemen's	gentleman's.

of great men, and remove them to a more fitting and more honourable resting-place. The Hôtel des Invalides at Paris, and the Basilica of San Lorenzo Fuori le Mura at Rome,* are indebted to this sentiment for the possession of relics which make those edifices the natural resort of pilgrims as of sight-seers. It were a work of superfluity to adduce further illustration of

* See *The Times*, July 14 and August 8, 1881.

SHAKESPEARE'S BONES.

THE sentiment which affects survivors in the disposition of their dead, and which is, in one regard, a superstition, is, in another, a creditable outcome of our common humanity: namely, the desire to honour the memory of departed worth, and to guard the "hallowed reliques" by the erection of a shrine, both as a visible mark of respect for the dead, and as a place of resort for those pilgrims who may come to pay him tribute. It is this sentiment which dots our graveyards with memorial tablets and more ambitious sculptures, and which still preserves so many of our closed churchyards from desecration, and its ancient tombs from the molestation of careless, curious, or mercenary persons.

But there is another sentiment, not inconsistent with this, which prompts us, on suitable occasions, to disinter the remains of great men, and remove them to a more fitting and more honourable resting-place. The Hôtel des Invalides at Paris, and the Basilica of San Lorenzo Fuori le Mura at Rome,* are indebted to this sentiment for the possession of relics which make those edifices the natural resort of pilgrims as of sight-seers. It were a work of superfluity to adduce further illustration of

* See *The Times*, July 14 and August 8, 1881.

the position that the mere exhumation and reinterment of a great man's remains, is commonly held to be, in special cases, a justifiable proceeding, not a violation of that honourable sentiment of humanity, which protects and consecrates the depositaries of the dead. On a late occasion it was not the belief that such a proceeding is a violation of our more sacred instincts which hindered the removal to Pennsylvania of the remains of William Penn; but simply the belief that they had already a more suitable resting-place in his native land.*

There is still another sentiment, honourable in itself and not inconsistent with those which I have specified, though still more conditional upon the sufficiency of the reasons conducing to the act: namely, the desire, by exhumation, to set at rest a reasonable or important issue respecting the person of the deceased while he was yet a living man. Accordingly it is held justifiable to exhume a body recently buried, in order to discover the cause of death, or to settle a question of disputed identity: nor is it usually held unjustifiable to exhume a body long since deceased, in order to find such evidences as time may not have wholly destroyed, of his personal appearance, including the size and shape of his head, and the special characteristics of his living face.

It is too late for the most reverential and scrupulous to object to this as an invasion of the sanctity of the grave, or a violation of the rights of the dead or of the feelings of his family. When a man has been long in the grave, there are probably no

* Jordan's Meeting-house, near Chalfort St. Giles, Bucks. See *The Times*, July 20, 1881.

family feelings to be wounded by such an act: and, as for his rights, if he can be said to have any, we may surely reckon among them the right of not being supposed to possess such objectionable personal defects as may have been imputed to him by the malice of critics or by the incapacity of sculptor or painter, and which his remains may be sufficiently unchanged to rebut: in a word we owe him something more than refraining from disturbing his remains until they are undistinguishable from the earth in which they lie, a debt which no supposed inviolable sanctity of the grave ought to present us from paying.

It is, I say, too late to raise such an objection, because exhumation has been performed many times with a perfectly legitimate object, even in the case of our most illustrious dead, without protest or objection from the most sensitive person. As the examples, more or less analogous to that of Shakespeare, which I am about to adduce, concern great men who were born and were buried within the limits of our island, I will preface them by giving the very extraordinary cases of Schiller and Raphael, which illustrate both classes: those in which the object of the exhumation was to give the remains a more honourable sepulture, and those in which it was purely to resolve certain questions affecting the skull of the deceased. The following is abridged from Mr. Andrew Hamilton's narrative, entitled "The Story of Schiller's Life," published in *Macmillan's Magazine* for May, 1863.

"At the time of his death Schiller left his widow and children almost penniless, and almost friendless too. The duke and duchess were absent; Goethe lay ill; even Schiller's brother- Schiller.

Schiller. in-law Wolzogen was away from home. Frau von Wolzogen was with her sister, but seems to have been equally ill-fitted to bear her share of the load that had fallen so heavily upon them. Heinrich Voss was the only friend admitted to the sick-room; and when all was over it was he who went to the joiner's, and, knowing the need of economy, ordered 'a plain deal coffin.' It cost ten shillings of our money.

In the early part of 1805, one Carl Leberecht Schwabe, an enthusiastic admirer of Schiller, left Weimar on business. Returning on Saturday the 11th of May, between three and four in the afternoon, his first errand was to visit his betrothed, who lived in the house adjoining that of the Schillers. She met him in the passage, and told him, Schiller was two days dead, and that night he was to be buried. On putting further questions, Schwabe stood aghast at what he learned. The funeral was to be private and to take place immediately after midnight, without any religious rite. Bearers had been hired to carry the remains to the churchyard, and no one else was to attend.

Schwabe felt that all this could not go on; but to prevent it was difficult. There were but eight hours left; and the arrangements, such as they were, had already been made. However, he went straight to the house of death, and requested an interview with Frau von Schiller. She replied, through the servant, 'that she was too greatly overwhelmed by her loss to be able to see or speak to any one; as for the funeral of her blessed husband, Mr. Schwabe must apply to the Reverend Oberconsistorialrath Günther, who had kindly undertaken to see done what was necessary; whatever he might direct, she would approve of.' With this message Schwabe hastened to Günther, and told him, his blood boiled at the thought that Schiller should be borne to the grave by hirelings. At first Günther shook his head and said, 'It was too late; everything was arranged; the bearers were already ordered.' Schwabe offered to become responsible for the payment of the bearers, if they were dismissed. At length the Oberconsistorialrath inquired who the gentlemen were who had agreed to bear the coffin. Schwabe was obliged to acknowledge that he could not at that moment mention a single name; but he was ready to guarantee his Hochwürde that in an hour or two he would bring him the list. On this his Hochwürde consented to countermand the bearers. Schiller.

Schwabe now rushed from house to house, obtaining a ready assent from all whom he found at home. But as some were out, he sent round a circular, begging those who would come to place a mark against their names. He requested them to meet at his lodgings 'at half-past twelve o'clock that night; a light would be placed in the window to guide those who were not acquainted with the house; they would be kind enough to be dressed in black; but mourning-hats, crapes and mantles he had already provided.' Late in the evening he placed the list in Günther's hands. Several appeared to whom he had not applied; in all about twenty.

Between midnight and one in the morning the little band proceeded to Schiller's house. The coffin was carried down stairs and placed on the shoulders of the friends in waiting. No one else was to be seen before the house or in the streets. It was a moonlight night in May, but clouds were up. The

Schiller. procession moved through the sleeping city to the churchyard of St. James. Having arrived there they placed their burden on the ground at the door of the so-called *Kassengewölbe*, where the gravedigger and his assistants took it up. In this vault, which belonged to the province of Weimar, it was usual to inter persons of the higher classes, who possessed no burying-ground of their own, upon payment of a *louis d'or*. As Schiller had died without securing a resting-place for himself and his family, there could have been no more natural arrangement than to carry his remains to this vault. It was a grim old building, standing against the wall of the churchyard, with a steep narrow roof, and no opening of any kind but the doorway which was filled up with a grating. The interior was a gloomy space of about fourteen feet either way. In the centre was a trap-door which gave access to a hollow space beneath.

As the gravediggers raised the coffin, the clouds suddenly parted, and the moon shed her light on all that was earthly of Schiller. They carried him in: they opened the trap-door: and let him down by ropes into the darkness. Then they closed the vault. Nothing was spoken or sung. The mourners were dispersing, when their attention was attracted by a tall figure in a mantle, at some distance in the graveyard, sobbing loudly. No one knew who it was; and for many years the occurrence remained wrapped in mystery, giving rise to strange conjectures. But eventually it turned out to have been Schiller's brother-in-law Wolzogen, who, having hurried home on hearing of the death, had arrived after the procession was already on its way to the churchyard.

In the year 1826, Schwabe was Bürgermeister of Weimar. Schiller. Now it was the custom of the *Landschaftscollegium*, or provincial board under whose jurisdiction this institution was placed, to *clear out* the Kassengewölbe from time to time—whenever it was found to be inconveniently crowded—and by this means to to make way for other deceased persons and more *louis d'or*. On such occasions—when the Landschaftscollegium gave the order 'aufzuräumen,' it was the usage to dig a hole in a corner of the churchyard—then to bring up *en masse* the contents of the Kassengewölbe—coffins, whether entire or in fragments, bones, skulls, and tattered graveclothes—and finally to shovel the whole heap into the aforesaid pit. In the month of March Schwabe was dismayed at hearing that the Landschaftscollegium had decreed a speedy 'clearing out' of the Gewölbe. His old prompt way of acting had not left him; he went at once to his friend Weyland, the president of the Collegium. 'Friend Weyland,' he said, 'let not the dust of Schiller be tossed up in the face of heaven and flung into that hideous hole! Let me at least have a permit to search the vault; if we find Schiller's coffin, it shall be reinterred in a fitting manner in the New Cemetery.' The president made no difficulty.

Schwabe invited several persons who had known the poet, and amongst others one Rudolph, who had been Schiller's servant at the time of his death. On March 13th, at four o'clock in the afternoon, the party met in the churchyard, the sexton and his assistants having received orders to be present with keys, ladders, &c. The vault was opened; but, before any one entered it, Rudolph and another stated that the

Schiller. coffin of the deceased Hofrath von Schiller must be one of the longest in the place. After this the secretary of the Landschaftscollegium was requested to read aloud from the records of the said board the names of such persons as had been interred shortly before and after the year 1805. This being done, the gravedigger Bielke remarked that the coffins no longer lay in the order in which they had originally been placed, but had been displaced at recent burials. The ladder was then adjusted, and Schwabe, Coudray the architect, and the gravedigger, were the first to descend. Some others were asked to draw near, that they might assist in recognising the coffin. The first glance brought their hopes very low. The tenants of the vault were found 'over, under and alongside of each other.' One coffin of unusual length having been descried underneath the rest, an attempt was made to reach it by lifting out of the way those that were above it; but the processes of the tomb were found to have made greater advances than met the eye. Hardly anything would bear removal, but fell to pieces at the first touch. Search was made for plates with inscriptions, but even the metal plates crumbled away on being fingered, and their inscriptions were utterly effaced. Two plates only were found with legible characters, and these were foreign to the purpose. Probably every one but the Bürgermeister looked on the matter as hopeless. They reascended the ladder and closed the vault.

Meanwhile these strange proceedings in the Kassengewölbe began to be noised abroad. The churchyard was a thoroughfare, and many passengers had observed that something unusual was going on. There were persons living in Weimar whose near relatives lay in the Gewölbe; and, though neither they nor the public at large had any objection to offer to the general 'clearing out,' they did raise very strong objections to this mode of anticipating it. So many pungent things began to be said about violating the tomb, disturbing the repose of the departed, &c., that the Bürgermeister perceived the necessity of going more warily to work in future. He resolved to time his next visit at an hour when few persons would be likely to cross the churchyard at that season. Accordingly, two days later he returned to the Kassengewölbe at seven in the morning, accompanied only by Coudray and the churchyard officials.

Schiller.

Their first task was to raise out of the vault altogether six coffins, which it was found would bear removal. By various tokens it was proved that none of these could be that of which they were in search. There were several others which could not be removed, but which held together so long as they were left where they lay. All the rest were in the direst confusion. Two hours and a half were spent in subjecting the ghastly heap to a thorough but fruitless search: not a trace of any kind rewarded their trouble. Only one conclusion stared Schwabe and Coudray in the face—their quest was in vain: the remains of Schiller must be left to oblivion. Again the Gewölbe was closed, and those who had disturbed its quiet returned disappointed to their homes. Yet, that very afternoon, Schwabe went back once more in company with the joiner who twenty years before had made the coffin: there was a chance that he might recognise one of those which they had not ventured to raise. But this

Schiller. glimmer of hope faded like all the rest. The man remembered very well what sort of coffin he had made for the Hofrath von Schiller, and he certainly saw nothing like it here. It had been of the plainest sort, he believed without even a plate; and in such damp as this it could have lasted but a few years.

The fame of this second expedition got abroad like that of the first, and the comments of the public were louder than before. Invectives of no measured sort fell on the mayor in torrents. Not only did society in general take offence, but a variety of persons in authority, particularly ecclesiastical dignitaries, began to talk of interfering. Schwabe was haunted by the idea of the 'clearing out,' which was now close at hand. That dismal hole in the corner of the churchyard once closed and the turf laid down, the dust of Schiller would be lost for ever. He determined to proceed. His position of Bürgermeister put the means in his power, and this time he was resolved to keep his secret. To find the skull was now his utmost hope, but for that he would make a final struggle. The keys were still in the hands of Bielke the sexton, who, of course, was under his control. He sent for him, bound him over to silence, and ordered him to be at the churchyard at midnight on the 19th of March. In like manner, he summoned three day-labourers whom he pledged to secrecy, and engaged to meet him at the same place and at the same hour, but singly and without lanterns. Attention should not be attracted if he could help it.

When the night came, he himself, with a trusty servant, proceeded to the entrance of the Kassengewölbe. The four men were already there. In darkness they all entered, raised the trap-door, adjusted the ladder, and descended to the abode of the dead. Not till then were lanterns lighted; it was just possible that some late wanderer might, even at that hour, cross the churchyard. Schwabe seated himself on a step of the ladder and directed the workmen. Fragments of broken coffins they piled up in one corner, and bones in another. Skulls as they were found were placed in a heap by themselves. The work went on from twelve o'clock till about three, for three successive nights, at the end of which time twenty-three skulls had been found. These the Bürgermeister caused to be put into a sack and carried to his house, where he himself took them out and placed them in rows on a table. Schiller.

It was hardly done ere he exclaimed, '*That* must be Schiller's!' There was one skull that differed enormously from all the rest, both in size and in shape. It was remarkable, too, in another way: alone of all those on the table it retained an entire set of the finest teeth, and Schiller's teeth had been noted for their beauty. But there were other means of identification at hand. Schwabe possessed the cast of Schiller's head, taken after death by Klauer, and with this he undertook to make a careful comparison and measurement. The two seemed to him to correspond, and, of the twenty-two others, not one would bear juxtaposition with the cast. Unfortunately the lower jaw was wanting, to obtain which a fourth nocturnal expedition had to be undertaken. The skull was carried back to the Gewölbe, and many jaws were tried ere one was found which fitted, and for beauty of teeth corresponded with, the upper jaw. When

Schiller. brought home, on the other hand, it refused to fit any other cranium. One tooth alone was wanting, and this was said by an old servant of Schiller's had been extracted at Jena in his presence.

Having got thus far, Schwabe invited three of the chief medical authorities to inspect his discovery. After careful measurements, they declared that among the twenty-three skulls there was but one from which the cast could have been taken. He then invited every person in Weimar and its neighbourhood, who had been on terms of intimacy with Schiller, and admitted them to the room one by one. The result was surprising. Without an exception they pointed to the same skull as that which must have been the poet's. The only remaining chance of mistake seemed to be the possibility of other skulls having eluded the search, and being yet in the vault. To put this to rest, Schwabe applied to the Landschaftscollegium, in whose records was kept a list of all persons buried in the Kassengewölbe. It was ascertained that since the last 'clearing out' there had been exactly twenty-three interments. At this stage the Bürgermeister saw himself in a position to inform the Grand Duke and Goethe of his search and its success. From both he received grateful acknowledgments. Goethe unhesitatingly recognised the head, and laid stress on the peculiar beauty and evenness of the teeth.

The new cemetery lay on a gently rising ground on the south side of the town. Schwabe's favourite plan was to deposit what he had found—all that he now ever dreamed of finding—of his beloved poet on the highest point of the slope, and to mark

Schiller.

the spot by a simple monument, so that travellers at their first approach might know where the head of Schiller lay. One forenoon in early spring he led Frau von Wolzogen and the Chancellor von Müller to the spot. They approved his plan, and the remaining members of Schiller's family—all of whom had left Weimar—signified their assent. They 'did not desire,' as one of themselves expressed it, 'to strive against Nature's appointment that man's earthly remains should be reunited with herself;' they would prefer that their father's dust should rest in the ground rather than anywhere else. But the Grand Duke and Goethe decided otherwise.

Dannecker's colossal bust of Schiller had recently been acquired for the Grand Ducal library, where it had been placed on a lofty pedestal opposite the bust of Goethe; and in this pedestal, which was hollow, it was resolved to deposit the skull. The consent of the family having been obtained, the solemnity was delayed till the arrival of Ernst von Schiller, who could not reach Weimar before autumn. On September the 17th the ceremony took place. A few persons had been invited, amongst whom, of course, was the Bürgermeister. Goethe, *more suo*, dreaded the agitation and remained at home, but sent his son to represent him as chief librarian. A cantata having been sung, Ernst von Schiller, in a short speech, thanked all persons present, but especially the Bürgermeister, for the love they had shown to the memory of his father. He then formally delivered his father's head into the hands of the younger Goethe, who, reverently receiving it, thanked his friend in Goethe's name, and having dwelt on the affection that had subsisted between their fathers

Schiller. vowed that the precious relic should thenceforward be guarded with anxious care. Up to this moment the skull had been wrapped in a cloth and sealed: the younger Goethe now made it over to the librarian, Professor Riemer, to be unpacked and placed in its receptacle. All present subscribed their names, the pedestal was locked, and the key carried home to Goethe.

None doubted that Schiller's head was now at rest for many years. But it had already occurred to Goethe, who had more osteological knowledge than the excellent Bürgermeister, that, the skull being in their possession, it would be possible to find the skeleton. A very few days after the ceremony in the library, he sent to Jena, begging the Professor of Anatomy, Dr. Schröter, to have the kindness to spend a day or two at Weimar, and to bring with him, if possible, a functionary of the Jena Museum, Färber by name, who had at one time been Schiller's servant. As soon as they arrived, Goethe placed the matter in Schröter's hands. Again the head was raised from its pillow and carried back to the dismal Kasselgewölbe, where the bones still lay in a heap. The chief difficulty was to find the first vertebra; after that all was easy enough. With some exceptions, comparatively trifling, Schröter succeeded in reproducing the skeleton, which then was laid in a new coffin 'lined with blue merino,' and would seem (though we are not distinctly told) to have been deposited in the library. Professor Schröter's register of bones recovered and bones missing has been both preserved and printed. The skull was restored to its place in the pedestal. There was another shriek from the public at these repeated violations of the tomb; and the odd position chosen for Schiller's head, apart from his body, called forth, not without reason, abundant criticism. Schiller.

Schwabe's idea of a monument in the new cemetery was, after a while, revived by the Grand Duke, Carl August, but with an important alteration, which was, that on the spot indicated at the head of the rising ground there should be erected a common sepulchre for Goethe and Schiller, in which the latter's remains should at once be deposited—the mausoleum to be finally closed only when, in the course of nature, Goethe should have been laid there too. The idea was, doubtless, very noble, and found great favour with Goethe himself, who entering into it commissioned Coudray, the architect, to sketch the plan of a simple mausoleum, in which the sarcophagi were to be visible from without. There was some delay in clearing the ground—a nursery of young trees had to be removed—so that at Midsummer, 1827, nothing had been done. It is said that the intrigues of certain persons, who made a point of opposing Goethe at all times, prevailed so far with the Grand Duke that he became indifferent about the whole scheme. Meanwhile it was necessary to provide for the remains of Schiller. The public voice was loud in condemning their present location, and in August, 1827, Louis of Bavaria again appeared as a *Deus ex machina* to hasten on the last act. He expressed surprise that the bones of Germany's best-beloved should be kept like rare coins, or other curiosities, in a public museum. In these circumstances, the Grand Duke wrote Goethe a note, proposing for his approval that the skull and skeleton of Schiller should be reunited and 'provisionally'

Schiller. deposited in the vault which the Grand Duke had built for himself and his house, 'until Schiller's family should otherwise determine.' No better plan seeming feasible, Goethe himself gave orders for the construction of a sarcophagus. On November 17th, 1827, in presence of the younger Goethe, Coudray and Riemer, the head was finally removed from the pedestal, and Professor Schröter reconstructed the entire skeleton in this new and more sumptuous abode, which we are told was seven feet in length, and bore at its upper end the name

SCHILLER

in letters of cast-iron. That same afternoon Goethe went himself to the library and expressed his satisfaction with all that had been done.

At last, on December 16th, 1827, at half-past five in the morning, a few persons again met at the same place. The Grand Duke had desired—for what reason we know not—to avoid observation; it was Schiller's fate that his remains should be carried hither and hither by stealth and in the night. Some tapers burned around the bier: the recesses of the hall were in darkness. Not a word was spoken, but those present bent for an instant in silent prayer, on which the bearers raised the coffin and carried it away. They walked along through the park: the night was cold and cloudy: some of the party had lanterns. When they reached the avenue that led up to the cemetery, the moon shone out as she had done twenty-two years before. At the vault itself some other friends had assembled, amongst whom was the Mayor. Ere the lid was finally secured, Schwabe placed himself at the head of the coffin, and recognised the skull to be that which he had rescued from the Kassengewölbe. The sarcophagus having then been closed, and a laurel wreath laid on it, formal possession, in the name of the Grand Duke, was taken by the Marshal, Freiherr von Spiegel. The key was removed to be kept in possession of his Excellency, the Geheimrath von Goethe, as head of the Institutions for Art and Science. This key, in an envelope, addressed by Goethe, is said to be preserved in the Grand Ducal Library, where, however, we have no recollection of having seen it.

Schiller.

The 'provisional' deposition has proved more permanent than any other. Whoever would see the resting-place of Goethe and Schiller must descend into the Grand Ducal vault, where, through a grating, in the twilight beyond he will catch a glimpse of their sarcophagi."

Raphael.

The other case of exhumation, and reinterment with funeral rites, which I deem of sufficient importance to be recorded here, is that of the great Raphael. In this the motive was not, as in that of Schiller, to give his bones a worthier resting-place, nor yet, as in so many other cases, to gratify a morbid curiosity, but to set at rest a question of disputed identity. In this respect the case of Raphael has a special bearing upon the matter in hand. I extract the following from *Mrs. Jameson's Lives of Italian Painters*, ed. 1874, p. 258:

"In the year 1833 there arose among the antiquarians of Rome a keen dispute concerning a human skull, which on no evidence whatever, except a long-received tradition, had been preserved and exhibited in the Academy of St. Luke as the

Raphael. skull of Raphael. Some even expressed a doubt as to the exact place of his sepulchre, though upon this point the contemporary testimony seemed to leave no room for uncertainty.

To ascertain the fact, permission was obtained from the Papal Government, and from the canons of the Church of the Rotunda (*i. e.*, of the Pantheon), to make some researches; and on the 14th of September in the same year, after five days spent in removing the pavement in several places, the remains of Raphael were discovered in a vault behind the high altar, and certified as his by indisputable proofs. After being examined, and a cast made from the skull and [one] from the right hand, the skeleton was exhibited publicly in a glass case, and multitudes thronged to the church to look upon it. On the 18th of October, 1833, a second funeral ceremony took place. The remains were deposited in a pine-wood coffin, then in a marble sarcophagus, presented by the Pope (Gregory XVI), and reverently consigned to their former resting-place, in presence of more than three thousand spectators, including almost all the artists, the officers of government, and other persons of the highest rank in Rome."

This event, as will appear in the sequel, is our best precedent for not permitting a sentimental respect for departed greatness to interfere with the respectful examination of a great man's remains, wherever such examination may determine a question to which "universal history is *not* indifferent."

Milton. Toland tells us that Milton's body was, on November 12, 1674, carried "to the Church of S. Giles, near *Cripplegate*, where he lies buried in the Chancel; and where the Piety of his Admirers will shortly erect a Monument becoming his worth, and the incouragement of Letters in King WILLIAM'S Reign."* It appears that his body was laid next to that of his father. A plain stone only was placed over the spot; and this, if Aubrey's account be trustworthy, was removed in 1679, when the two steps were raised which lead to the altar. The remains, however, were undisturbed for nearly sixteen years. On the 4th of August, 1790, according to a small volume written by Philip Neve, Esq. (of which two editions were published in the same year), Milton's coffin was removed, and his remains exhibited to the public on the 4th and 5th of that month. Mr. George Steevens, the great editor of Shakespeare, who justly denounced the indignity *intended*, not offered, to the great Puritan poet's remains by Royalist landsharks, satisfied himself that the corpse was that of a woman of fewer years than Milton. Thus did good Providence, or good fortune, defeat the better half of their nefarious project: and I doubt not their gains were spent as money is which has been "gotten over the devil's back." Steevens' assurance gives us good reason for believing that Mr. Philip Neve's indignant protest is only good in the general, and that Milton's "hallowed reliques" still "rest undisturb'd within their peaceful shrine." I have adduced this instance to serve as an example of what I condemn, and should, in any actual case, denounce as strongly as Mr. Philip Neve or George Steevens. To expose a man's remains after any interval for the purpose of treating his memory with indignity, or of denouncing an unpopular cause which he espoused, or (worst of all) "to

Milton.

* *The Life of Milton.* London: 1699. P. 149.

Milton. fine his bones," or make money by the public exhibition of his dust, deserves unmeasured and unqualified reprobation, and every prudent measure should be taken to render such an act impossible.

Cromwell. To take another example of the reprehensible practice of despoiling the grave of a great enemy: Oliver Cromwell was, as is proved by the most reliable evidence, namely, that of a trustworthy eye-witness, buried on the scene of his greatest achievement, the Field of Naseby. Some Royalist *Philister* is said to have discovered, and stolen from its resting-place, the embalmed head of the great Protector. It found its way to London towards the end of the last century, where it was exhibited at No. 5, Mead Court, Old Bond Street.* It is said to have been acquired by Sir Joshua Reynolds in September, 1786, and to be now or late in the collection of Mr. W. A. Wilkinson, of Beckenham. It is recorded in one of the *Additional Manuscripts* in the British Museum, under date April 21, 1813, that "an offer was made this morning to bring it to Soho Square, to show it to Sir Joseph Banks, but he desired to be excused from seeing *the remains of the old villanous Republican, the mention of whose very name makes his blood boil with indignation.* The same offer was made to Sir Joseph forty years ago, which he also refused." What a charming specimen was Banks of the genus Tory! But after all it is a comfort to think that on this occasion he was right: for while this head was undoubtedly that which did duty for the Protector at Tyburn, and was afterwards fixed on the top

* *Morning Chronicle*, March 18, 1799.

of Westminster Hall, it was almost certainly not that of Oliver Cromwell: whose remains probably still lie crumbling into dust in their unknown grave on Naseby Field.* Cromwell.

Swedenborg.

I give one more example of robbing the grave of an illustrious man, through the superstition of many and the cupidity of one. Swedenborg was buried in the vault of the Swedish Church in Prince's Square, on April 5, 1772. In 1790, in order to determine a question raised in debate, viz., whether Swedenborg were really dead and buried, his wooden coffin was opened, and the leaden one was sawn across the breast. A few days after, a party of Swedenborgians visited the vault. "Various relics" (says White: *Life of Swedenborg*, 2nd ed., 1868, p. 675) "were carried off: Dr. Spurgin told me he possessed the cartilage of an ear. Exposed to the air, the flesh quickly fell to dust, and a skeleton was all that remained for subsequent visitors. * * At a funeral in 1817, Granholm, an officer in the Swedish Navy, seeing the lid of Swedenborg's coffin loose, abstracted the skull, and hawked it about amongst London Swedenborgians, but none would buy. Dr. Wählin, pastor of the Swedish Church, recovered what he supposed to be the stolen skull, had a cast of it taken, and placed it in the coffin in 1819. The cast which is sometimes seen in phrenological collections is obviously not Swedenborg's: it is thought to be that of a small female skull."

Charles I.

In the latter part of the reign of George III a mausoleum was built in the Tomb House at Windsor Castle. On its completion, in the spring of 1813, it was determined to open a passage of

* See *Notes and Queries*, 1st S., xi, 496, and xii, 75.

Charles I. communication with St. George's Chapel, and in constructing this an opening was accidentally made in one of the walls of the vault of Henry VIII, through which the workmen could see three coffins, one of which was covered with a black velvet pall. It was known that Henry VIII and Queen Jane Seymour were buried in this vault, but a question had been raised as to the place of Charles the First's interment, though the statement of Lord Clarendon, that the search made for the late King's coffin at Windsor (with a view to its removal to Westminster Abbey) had proved fruitless. Sir Henry Halford, in his *Account*, appended to his *Essays and Orations*, 1831,* thus describes the examination of the palled coffin.

"On representing the circumstance to the Prince Regent, his R. H. perceived at once that *a doubtful point in history might be cleared up by opening this vault;* and accordingly his R. H. ordered an examination to be made on the first convenient opportunity. This was done on the First of April last [*i. e.*, 1813], the day after the funeral of the Duchess of Brunswick, in the presence of his R. H. himself, who guaranteed thereby *the most respectful care and attention to the remains of the dead*, during the enquiry. His R. H. was accompanied by his R. H. the Duke of Cumberland, Count Munster, the Dean of Windsor, Benjamin Charles Stevenson, Esq., and Sir Henry Halford."

The vault was accordingly further opened and explored, and the palled coffin, which was of lead, and bore the inscription

* *An Account of what appeared on opening the Coffin of King Charles the First in the vault of Henry VIII, in* [*the Tomb House,*] *St. George's Chapel, Windsor, on the First of April, MDCCCXIII.*

'King Charles, 1648,' was opened at the head. A second coffin of wood was thus disclosed, and, through this, the body carefully wrapped up in cere-cloth, into the folds of which a quantity of unctuous or greasy matter, mixed with resin, as it seemed, had been melted, so as to exclude, as effectually as possible, the external air. The coffin was completely full; and, from the tenacity of the cere-cloth, great difficulty was experienced in detaching it successfully from the parts which it enveloped. Wherever the unctuous matter had insinuated itself, the separation of the cere-cloth was easy; and when it came off, a correct impression of the features to which it had been applied was observed in the unctuous substance.* At length the whole face was disengaged from its covering. The complexion of the skin was dark and discoloured. The forehead and temples had lost little or nothing of their muscular substance; the cartilage of the nose was gone; but the left eye, in the first moment of exposure, was open and full, though it vanished almost immediately: and the pointed beard, so characteristic of the reign of King Charles, was perfect. The shape of the face was a long oval; many of the teeth remained; and the left ear, in consequence of the interposition of the unctuous matter between it and the cere-cloth, was found entire." Charles I.

The head was found to be loose, and was once more held up to view; and after a careful examination of it had been made, and a sketch taken, and the identity fully established, it was

* It appears that the examiners omitted to utilize this unctuous mask for the purpose of taking a plaster cast: a default which, as we shall see, has been paralleled by those who conducted other examinations of the kind.

Charles I. immediately replaced in the coffin, which was soldered up and restored to the vault. Of the other two coffins, the larger one had been battered in about the middle, and the skeleton of Henry VIII, exhibiting some beard upon the chin, was exposed to view. The other coffin was left, as it was found, intact. Neither of these coffins bore any inscription.

Burns. In the Appendix to Allan Cunningham's *Life of Burns** we read of an examination of the poet's Tomb, made immediately after that life was published:

"When Burns' Mausoleum was opened in March, 1834, to receive the remains of his widow, some residents in Dumfries obtained the consent of her nearest relative to take a cast from the cranium of the poet. This was done during the night between the 31st March and 1st April. Mr. Archibald Blacklock, surgeon, drew up the following description:

"'The cranial bones were perfect in every respect, if we except a little erosion of their external table, and firmly held together by their sutures, &c., &c. Having completed our intention [*i. e.*, of taking a plaster cast of the skull, washed from every particle of sand, &c.], the skull, securely closed in a leaden case, was again committed to the earth, precisely where we found it.—Archd. Blacklock.'"

Jonson. The last example I shall adduce is that of Ben Jonson's skull. On this Lieut.-Colonel Cunningham thus writes:

"In my boyhood I was familiar with the Abbey, and well remember the 'pavement square of blew marble, 14 inches square, with O RARE BEN JONSON,' which marked the poet's grave. When Buckland was Dean, the spot had to be disturbed

* *Works of Robert Burns:* Bohn, 1842.

for the coffin of Sir Robert Wilson, and the Dean sent his son Frank, now so well known as an agreeable writer on Natural History, to see whether he could observe anything to confirm, or otherwise, the tradition about Jonson being buried in a standing posture. The workmen, he tells us, 'found a coffin very much decayed, which from the appearance of the remains must have originally been placed in the upright position. The skull found among these remains, Spice, the gravedigger, gave me as that of Ben Jonson, and I took it at once into the Dean's study. We examined it together, and then going into the Abbey carefully returned it to the earth.' In 1859, when John Hunter's coffin was removed to the Abbey, the same spot had to be dug up, and Mr. Frank Buckland again secured the skull of Jonson, placing it at the last moment on the coffin of the great surgeon. So far, so good; but not long afterwards, a statement appeared in the 'Times' that the skull of Ben Jonson was in the possession of a blind gentleman at Stratford-upon-Avon. Hereupon Mr. Buckland made further inquiries, and calmly tells us that he has convinced himself that the skull which he had taken such care of on two occasions, [such care as not so much as to measure or sketch it!] was not Jonson's skull at all; that a Mr. Ryde had anticipated him both times in removing and replacing the genuine article, [!] and that the Warwickshire claimant [!] was a third skull which Mr. Ryde observed had been purloined from the grave on the second opening. Mr. Buckland is a scientific naturalist, and an ardent worshipper of the closest of all observers, John Hunter. Now mark what satisfies such a man on such an occasion as this. He was wrong and Mr. Ryde was right,

Jonson.

Jonson. because Mr. Ryde described *his* skull as having *red hair;* and in Aubrey's *Lives of Eminent Men*, 'I find evidence quite sufficient for any medical man to come to the conclusion that Ben Jonson's hair was in all probability of a red colour, though the fact *is not stated in so many words.*' In so many words! I think not! Actually all that Aubrey says on the subject is, '*He was, or rather had been, of a cleare and faire skin*'! (*Lives*, ii, 414.) And this, too, in spite of our knowing from his own pen, and from more than one painting, that his hair was as black as the raven's wing! Besides, he was sixty-five years old when he died, and we may be sure that the few locks he had left were neither red nor black, but of the hue of the 'hundred of grey hairs' which he described as remaining eighteen years before. Mr. Buckland's statement will be found in the *Fourth Series* of his *Curiosities of Natural History*, one of the most entertaining little volumes with which we are acquainted." *

In reviewing the various incidents connected with the foregoing cases of exhumation one is perhaps most struck with the last two. That an illustrious man of science, and his son, who at that time must already have been a scientific naturalist, should have coöperated in so stupendous a blunder as the mere inspection of Ben Jonson's skull, without taking so much as a measurement or drawing of it, would be incredible, but for the fact that both are dead, and nothing of the sort has come to light: and it is scarcely less surprising that the Swedenborgians,

* Prefatory Notice to Cunningham's larger edition of Ben Jonson's Works, pp. xviii—xx. For other examples, see *God's Acre*, by Mrs. Stone, 1858, chapter xiv, and *Notes and Queries*, 6th S., vii, 161.

who believed themselves to be in possession of their founder's skull, should not have left on record some facts concerning its shape and size.

Bacon.

Before addressing myself to the principal matter of this essay, namely the question whether we should not attempt to recover Shakespeare's skull, I may as well note, that the remains of the great philosopher, whom so many regard as Shakespeare's very self, or else his *alter ego*, were not allowed to remain unmolested in their grave in St. Michael's Church, St. Albans. Thomas Fuller, in his *Worthies*, relates as follows: "Since I have read that his grave being occasionally opened [!] his scull (the relique of civil veneration) was by one King, a Doctor of Physick, made the object of scorn and contempt; but he who then derided the dead has since become the laughingstock of the living." This, being quoted by a correspondent in *Notes and Queries*,* elicited from Mr. C. Le Poer Kennedy, of St. Albans,† an account of a search that had been made for Bacon's remains, on the occasion of the interment of the last Lord Verulam. "A partition wall was pulled down, and the search extended into the part of the vault immediately under the monument, but no remains were found." On the other hand, we have the record of his express wish to be buried there. I am afraid the doctor, who is said to have become the laughingstock of the living, has entirely faded out of men's minds and memories.

Among the many protests against the act of exhumation, I select that of Capel Lofft, as representative of the rest. He writes—

* 2nd S., viii, 354. † *Ibid*, ix, 132.

"It were to be wished that neither superstition, affectation, idle curiosity, or avarice, were so frequently invading the silence of the grave. Far from dishonouring the illustrious dead, it is rather outraging the common condition of humanity, and last melancholy state in which our present existence terminates. Dust and ashes have no intelligence to give, whether beauty, genius, or virtue, informed the animated clay. A tooth of Homer or Milton will not be distinguished from one of a common mortal; nor a bone of Alexander acquaint us with more of his character than one of Bucephalus. Though the dead be unconcerned, the living are neither benefited nor improved: decency is violated, and a kind of instinctive sympathy infringed, which, though it ought not to overpower reason, ought not without it, and to no purpose, to be superseded." Notwithstanding the right feeling shewn in this passage, it is quite sufficient to condemn Capel Lofft as a *Philister.* Let us for a moment examine some of these very eloquent assertions. Agreeing as I cordially do with his wish, that neither superstition, affectation, whatever that may mean, idle curiosity, or avarice, were the motives which actuate those who molest the relics of the dead, I cannot allow that neither dust and ashes, bones, nor teeth, have any intelligence to give us; nor yet that by the reverential scrutiny of those relics the living can be neither benefited nor improved. All that depends upon the intelligence of the scrutineer. Doubtless your *Philister* would turn over the skull or the bones, or make hay with the dust, just as Peter Bell could see nothing in a primrose but a weed in flower. What message a bone or a weed may have for the man or the race depends wholly upon the recipient. Your Shakespeare or Goethe, your Owen or Huxley, would find in it an intelligible language; while your Capel Lofft would denounce what he found there as dirt and indecency. How true is the proverb of Syr Oracle Mar-text: "To the wise all things are wise." In the case of Schiller, the skull spoke for itself, and claimed to be that of Schiller; the bones, like those in the 37th chapter of *Ezekiel*, aggregated themselves around their head, and submitted to an accurate articulation; and the teeth gave their evidence, too, at least the place of one, which was not in the jaw, bore its testimony to the fact that the jaw in question was that which Schiller had submitted to dentistry. In the case of Raphael, the discovery of the skull disproved the claims of the spurious relic, and arrested a stupid superstition.* Beyond question, the skull of Shakespeare, might we but discover it in anything like its condition at the time of its interment, would be of still greater interest and value. It would at least settle two disputed points in the Stratford Bust; it would test the Droeshout print, and every one of the half-dozen portraits-in-oils which pass as presentments of Shakespeare's face at different periods of his life. Moreover it would pronounce decisively on the pretensions of the Kesselstadt Death-Mask, and we should know whether that was from the "flying-mould" after which Gerard Johnson worked, when he sculptured the Bust. Negative evidence the skull would

* The case of Dante has been recently alluded to, as if it were one of exhumation. But despite the efforts of the Florentines to recover the remains of their great poet, they still rest at Ravenna, in the grave in which they were deposited immediately after his death.

assuredly furnish; but there is reason for believing that it would afford positive evidence in favour of the Bust, one or other of the portraits, or even of the Death-Mask: and why, I ask, should not an attempt be made to recover Shakespeare's skull? Why should not the authorities of Stratford, to whom this brochure is inscribed, sanction, or even themselves undertake, a respectful examination of the grave in which Shakespeare's remains are believed to have been buried?

Two grounds have always been assigned for abstention: (1) the sentiment which disposes men to leave the relics of the dead to their rest in the tomb: (2) the prohibition contained in the four lines inscribed upon Shakespeare's gravestone. With the former of these I have sufficiently dealt already. As for the latter; the prohibitory lines, whether they proceeded from our Poet himself, as Mr. William Page, and many before him, believed, or from the pen of Ben Jonson, or of an inferior writer (which is to me the more probable authorship), I am most desirous to respect them; not that I stand in awe of Shakespeare's curse, but because I think they proceeded from a natural and laudable fear. I have no more doubt that "moves," in the quatrain, means "*re*moves," than I have that "stones" means "*grave*stones." The fear which dictated these curious lines, was, I believe, lest Shakespeare's remains should be carried, whither so many of his predecessors in the church-yard had been carried, to the common charnel-house hard-by. I do not read in those lines a prohibition against an examination of the grave, say for purposes of knowledge and history, but against the despoiling of that grave, to make room for some local knight, squire, or squireen, who might have been deemed a worthier tenant of the Chancel room. Shakespeare's body was carried to the grave on Thursday, April 25, 1616 (O. S.); and, beyond question, his son-in-law, Dr. John Hall, made all the arrangements, and bore all the expenses. We have no proof whatever that the grave has remained closed from that time: on the contrary there is some slight *scintilla* of proof that it has been explored; and it would never astonish me to learn that Shakespeare's skull had been abstracted! There may yet be some among us who have a personal interest in preventing such an exploration, and in thus maintaining the general belief, that Shakespeare's relics still rest in the mould in which they were buried.

Be that as it may: in the year 1796, the supposed grave was actually broken into, in the course of digging a vault in its immediate proximity; and not much more than fifty years ago the slab over the grave, having sunk below the level of the pavement, was removed, the surface was levelled, and a fresh stone was laid over the old bed. It is certain, I believe, that the original stone did not bear the name of Shakespeare, any more than its successor: but it is not certain that the four lines appear upon the new stone in exactly the same literal form as they did upon the old one.* I wish I could add that these two were the only occasions when either grave or grave-stone was meddled with. I am informed, on the authority of a Free and Accepted Mason, that a Brother-Mason of

* *Traditionary Anecdotes of Shakespeare.* 1883, p. 11.

his has explored the grave which purports to be Shakespeare's, and that he found nothing in it but dust. The former statement must be taken *cum grano.* Granting this, however, the latter statement will not surprise my valued friend Mr. J. O. Halliwell-Phillipps, who thinks he sees a reason for the disappearance of SHAKESPEARE'S BONES, in the fact that his coffin was buried in the Chancel mould.* If this be all the ground of his assurance, that nothing but dust would reward the search, I would say "despair thy charm;" for many corpses so buried have for many years been preserved in comparative freshness—corpses which had been treated with no more care than the body of Shakespeare is believed to have received. The last case to come to my knowledge, was that of the Birmingham poet, John Freeth, the father of my old friend John Freeth, formerly the Clerk (or principal manager) of the Birmingham Canal Navigations. On the destruction of the burial-place of the Old Meeting House, in Old Meeting Street, Birmingham, in March, 1882, the coffin of the poet was found in the earth, and on opening it, the face was almost as fresh, and quite as perfect, as on the day of the old man's interment seventy-four years before: and as to his bones? Does Mr. Halliwell-Phillipps believe that in a period but little more than double that of the poet Freeth's unmolested repose, namely 180 years, all SHAKESPEARE'S BONES would have been turned to dust, and become indistinguishable from the mould in which the coffin lay? To ask this question is to answer it. A more

* *Outlines of the Life of Shakespeare.* 3rd edition, 1883, p. 223.

credulous man, than I know Mr. Halliwell-Phillipps to be, would hesitate to give an affirmative answer. Depend upon it, Shakespeare's skull is in his grave, unchanged; or it has been abstracted. There may well have been a mistake as to the exact locality of the grave: for we do not know that the new gravestone was laid down exactly over the place of the one that was removed; and the skull may be found in a grave hard-by. But if, on making a thorough search, no skull be found, I shall believe that it has been stolen: for, apart from the fact of its non-discovery, I should almost be disposed to say, that no superstition, or fear of Shakespeare's curse, nor any official precaution and vigilance, could have been a match for that combination of curiosity, cupidity, and relic-worship, which has so often prompted and carried out the exhumation of a great man's bones. If there were no other reason for searching Shakespeare's grave, save the extinction of an unpleasant but not irrational doubt, I would forthwith perform the exploration, and if possible obtain tangible proof that the poet's skull had not been removed from its resting-place.

But the exploration, if successful, would have a bearing upon more material issues. The most opposite judgments have been passed upon the Bust, both as a work of art and as a copy of nature. Landor, whose experience of Italian art was considerable, recorded it as his opinion, that it was the noblest head ever sculptured; while Mr. Hain Friswell depreciated it, declaring it to be "rudely cut and heavy, without any feeling, a mere block": smooth and round like a boy's marble.* After

* *Life Portraits of Shakespeare.* 1864, p. 10.

some of Mr. Friswell's deliverances, I am not disposed to rank his judgment very high; and I accept Landor's decision. As to the finish of the face, Mr. Fairholt's criticism is an exaggeration, successfully exposed by Mr. Friswell. My own opinion, *telle quelle*, has been already printed.* Allowing the bust to have been a recognisable, if not a staring likeness of the poet, I said and still say—"How awkward is the *ensemble* of the face! What a painful stare, with its goggle eyes and gaping mouth! The expression of this face has been credited with *humour, bonhommie* and *jollity*. To me it is decidedly *clownish;* and is suggestive of a man crunching a sour apple, or struck with amazement at some unpleasant spectacle. Yet there is force in the lineaments of this muscular face." The large photograph of the Monument lately issued by the *New Shakspere Society*, as well as those more successful issues of Mr. Thrupp's studio, fully bears out this judgment. But the *head*, as Landor said, is noble. Without accepting the suggestion that the sculptor had met with an accident to the nose, and had, in consequence, to lengthen the upper lip, I think it self-evident that there is some little derangement of natural proportions in those features; the nose, especially, being ill-formed and undersized for the rest of the face. If we had but Shakespeare's skull before us, most of these questions would be set at rest for ever.

Among the relics once religiously preserved in the Kesselstadt collection at Mayence was a plaster mask, having at the back the year of Shakespeare's death. This relic had been in

* *Shakespeare: The Man and The Book. Part I*, p. 79.

that collection time out of mind, and seems always to have been received as a cast from the "flying-mould" of Shakespeare's dead face. With this was a small oil-painting of a man crowned with bays, lying on a state bier; of which, by the kindness of Mr. J. Parker Norris of Philadelphia, I am able to give the admirable engraving which forms the frontispiece to this little volume. On the death of Count and Canon Francis von Kesselstadt, at Mayence, in 1843, the family museum was broken up, and its contents dispersed. No more was seen or heard of either of the two relics described, till 1847, when the painting was purchased by an artist named Ludwig Becker; and after some months of unremitting search he discovered the Death-Mask in a broker's shop, and this he bought in 1849. The purchaser is dead: but both these relics are in the Grand Ducal Museum at Darmstadt, and belong to its curator, Dr. Ernst Becker, Ludwig's brother. I have inspected both with the keenest interest; and I am of opinion that the painting is not after the mask. The date, 1637, which it bears, led Dr. Schaafhausen to think that it was intended for Ben Jonson; a view to some extent borne out by the portrait of Ben in the Dulwich Gallery.* By others, however, it is believed to be a fancy portrait of Shakespeare, based upon the Death-Mask. Now the Bust was believed to have been sculptured after a death-mask. Is the Becker Mask that from which Gerard Johnson worked? If so, there must have been a fatal accident indeed to the nose; for the nose of the

* As to this, see an article contributed by me to *The Antiquary* for September, 1880: also the *Shakespeare Jahrbuch*, vol. x, 1875, for Dr. Schaafhausen's views.

mask is a long and finely arched one: the upper lip is shorter than that of the bust, and the forehead is more receding.

Of the many alleged portraits of Shakespeare there are but two whose pedigree stretches back into the seventeenth century, and is lost in obscurity there. The origin of the vast majority of the claimants is only too well known, or shrewdly suspected: these are (1) copies, more or less unfaithful, of older pictures; (2) idealised portraits, based upon such older ones, or upon the Bust; (3) genuine portraits of unknown persons, valued for some slight or imaginary resemblance to the Bust, or to such older portraits, or for having passed as Shakespeare's, and thus offering the means of selling dear what had been bought cheap; (4) impostures. As I am not writing an essay upon the portraits, I will merely mention in the order of their importance the few claimants whose title merits the least consideration.

I.—The Droeshout engraving, prefixed to the first collective edition of the Poet's works, published in 1623: *i. e.*, the print in its early state.

II.—The so-called Janssen portrait (on wood) in the collection of the Duke of Somerset, at Sherburn Castle, Dorset. This has been traced back to 1761, when it was purchased by Charles Jennens, Esq., of Gopsall. Its identity with the portrait which was purchased for the Duke of Hamilton and Brandon in 1809 is, at least, highly probable. In 1811 Woodburn published the first engraving from it, and stated that the picture had belonged to Prince Rupert, who left it to Mrs. E. S. Howes on his death in 1682. No actual proof of this was given, nor did Woodburn mention Jennens' ownership.

III.—The Croker portrait. We have it on the authority of Boaden that this portrait, which he said was the property of the Right Hon. J. Wilson Croker, was a replica of the Janssen. There was a mystery, not in the least cleared up, concerning these two pictures and their history. I am unable to ascertain who at present owns the latter. Collectors of the prints can always distinguish between the two. The only engraving of the Croker portrait was by R. Cooper; published January 1, 1824, by G. Smeeton, and is an oval in a shaded rectangle. All the rest are either from the Janssen, or from Dunkarton's engraving of it.*

IV.—The Chandos portrait (on wood) in the National Portrait Gallery at South Kensington. It has been traced back to 1668, when, on Davenant's death, it passed to John Otway: but not in its present or even late condition.

V.—The Lumley portrait, well known through the admirable chromo-lithograph, by Mr. Vincent Brooks (which is scarcely distinguishable from the original), and once sold for forty guineas as the original portrait. It has been traced back to 1785.

* There is no engraving by "Dunbar": that name was Friswell's mistake for Dunkarton. Boaden's "absolute fac-simile" and "no difference whatever," (*Inquiry*, l. p., page 137) are expressions not borne out by the engravings. My old friend, the Rev. Charles Evans, Rector of Solihull, who possesses the almost unrivalled Marsh Collection of Engraved Portraits of Shakespeare, at my request compared Cooper's engraving of the Croker portrait with those by Dunkarton, Earlom, and Turner, of the Janssen: and he writes: "In the Cooper the face is peaked, the beard more pointed, and the ruff different in the points." After all, such differences may well be the creation of the engravers. I would fain know where the Croker portrait now is; and also that which belonged to the late Dr. Turton, Bishop of Ely.

VI.—The Ashbourne portrait.

VII.—The Felton portrait (on wood), traced back to 1792.

VIII.—The Challis portrait (on wood).

IX.—The Hunt portrait: at the Birthplace. This is not in its original state, and cannot be judged-of apart from a copy of it in the possession of John Rabone, Esq., of Birmingham.

Of these III, VI, and VIII have not been satisfactorily traced back even into the last century.

Beyond question, after the Bust and the Droeshout engraving, the Janssen portrait has the greatest value. Unfortunately the Chandos, even if its history be as stated, is of very little real value: for it has been so often repaired or "restored," and is at present in such a dilapidated condition, that it cannot be relied upon as a portrait. Moreover it bears but little resemblance to the admirable drawing from it in its former state, made by Ozias Humphreys in the year 1783. This drawing is an exceedingly fine work of art, to which even Scriven's print, good as it is, scarcely does justice. To compare Humphreys' drawing, which hangs in the Birthplace, and is its most valuable portrait, with Samuel Cousin's fine mezzotint of the Chandos, engraved forty years ago, is to be convinced that the existing picture no longer represents the man—whosoever he may have been—from whom it was painted. How many questions, affecting the Bust, the Death-Mask, and these portraits, would not be set at rest by the production of Shakespeare's skull!

The late Mr. William Page, the American sculptor, whose interest in testing the identity of the Kesselstadt Death-Mask, by comparing it with Shakespeare's skull, was in 1874-5 incomparably greater than that of any other interested person, comes *very near* the expression of a wish for the exhumation of the skull.* But he had not the courage to express that wish, and after the passage which I am about to quote, abruptly changes the subject. He says, "The man who wrote the four lines [of epitaph] which have thus far secured his bones that rest which his epitaph demands, omitted nothing likely to carry the whole plan into effect. The authorship of the epitaph cannot be doubted, unless another man in England had the wit and wisdom to divine the loyal heart's core of its people, and touch it in the single appeal 'for Jesus sake.' Nothing else has kept him out of Westminster [Abbey]. The style of the command and curse are Shakespearian, and triumphant as any art of forethought in his plays." Then follows on—without even the break of a paragraph—not what naturally should have followed, and *must* have been in Mr. Page's mind, but a citation of Chantrey and John Bell, as to the model from which the Bust was made. Possibly it is due to the omission of a sentence, which once intervened between the remarks on the remains and those which concern the Bust of Shakespeare, that we have now two totally different matters in juxtaposition, and in the same paragraph. In this Death-Mask Mr. Page saw the reconciliation of the Bust, the Droeshout print (in its best state), and the Chandos portrait. I do not meddle with that opinion, or the evidences upon which it rests. But I have inspected all the four: I have also seen Mr. Page's life-size bronze bust, and wish I had never

* *A Study of Shakespeare's Portraits.* 1876, p. 23.

seen it, or even a photograph of it, for it destroyed for me a pleasant dream.

But whatever be the value of Mr. Page's conclusion, or of his Bust, I have no doubt that the value of his book lies in those accurate "Dimensions of Shakespeare's Mask," which he took during his six days of free access to the Grand Ducal Museum. The measurements are on pp. 51—55 of his book, and may eventually be of the greatest possible use, if the time should ever arrive when Shakespeare's skull will be subjected to similar measurement. For myself, I am disposed to believe that no mistaken sense of duty on the part of the Stratford authorities will long be able to prevent that examination, if the skull be still in existence.

A Bibliography

OF

THE EXHUMATION QUESTION

AS AFFECTING

SHAKESPEARE'S BONES.

—o—

1.—HAWTHORNE, NATHANIEL, in "Recollections of a Gifted Woman," in *Our Old Home* (reprinted from the *Atlantic Monthly*, January, 1863), records Miss Delia Bacon's project for exploring Shakespeare's grave, and the failure of her attempt through the irresolution occasioned by her fear of disappointment.

2.—NORRIS, J. PARKER, in the New York *American Bibliopolist*, of April, 1876, vol. viii, p. 38, in the section entitled "Shakspearian Gossip" [reprinted in the Philadelphia *Press*, August 4, 1876], seriously proposes the exhumation of Shakespeare's remains, and asks, "Is it not worth making an effort to secure 'the counterfeit presentment' of him who wrote 'for all time'? If we could even get a photograph of Shakspeare's skull it would be a great thing, and would help us to make a better portrait of him than we now possess." His courageous article is particularly useful for the adduction of cases in which corpses have lain in the grave far longer than that of Shakespeare, and been discovered in a state of comparative perfection. What would one not give to look upon Shakespeare's dead face!

The letter of "a friend residing near Stratford," from which he gives a long extract, was from one of my present colleagues in the Shakespeare Trust, viz.:

3.—TIMMINS, SAM., as quoted in the last recorded article, writes—"Some graves of the Shakspeare date were opened at Church Lawford a few years ago, and the figures, faces, and dresses were perfect, but, of course, in half an hour were mere heaps of dust. Shakspeare's grave is near the Avon, but doubtless he was buried well (in a leaden coffin probably), and there is scarcely room for a doubt that, with proper precautions, photographs of his face might be taken perfectly. Surely the end does justify the means here. It is not to satisfy mere idle curiosity. It is not mere relic-mongering; it is simply to secure for posterity what we could give—an exact representation of the great poet as he lived and died. Surely this is justifiable, at least it is allowable, in the absence of any authentic portrait. Surely such a duty might be most reverently done. I doubt after all if it will be; but I am very strongly in favour of the trial, and if no remains were found, no harm would be done, the 'curse' to the contrary notwithstanding. People who have pet projects about portraits would not like to have all their neat and logical arguments knocked on the head, but where *should* we *all* be if no Shakspeare at all were found, but only a bundle of musty old MSS. in Lord Bacon's 'fine Roman hand'? After all, I am rather nervous about the result of such an exhumation. But, seriously, I see no reason why it should not be made. A legal friend here long ago suggested (humorously, not professionally of course) that the 'curse' might be escaped by employing a woman ('cursed be *he*') and women would compete for the honor!"

4.—Anonymous Article in *The Birmingham Daily Mail*, of August 23, 1876, headed "Shakspeare's *Carte de Visite*." This is strongly adverse to Mr. Norris's proposals. The writer inclines to believe that the "friend residing near Stratford" was "a fiction of the Mrs. Harris type," or "possibly a modest way of evading the praise which would be the meed of the brilliant genius who originated the project": both very random guesses, and, as it turns out, wide of the mark. The article ends thus: "If Moses had been raised in Massachussetts he would have been wanted to take a camera or some business-cards up Sinai." For our part, if we shall be so fortunate as to find Shakespeare alive in his grave, we shall of course raise him, and invite him to coöperate in the business of photographing his own shining face. But we are not so sanguine as to expect that miracle, though almost as great wonders have been done by the power of this magician. But where is the "triple curse" with which, according to this authority, "that gravestone is weighted"? Quite another view of the inscription is given by Lord Ronald Gower, *infra*.

5.—Anonymous Article in the London *Daily Telegraph*, of August 24, 1876: also strongly adverse to Mr. Norris.

6.—Schaafhausen, Hermann, in the *Jahrbuch*, or Annual, of the German Shakespeare Society, vol. x, 1875, asks: "Should we be afraid to rely on this evidence [agreement of Mask with known portraits, &c.], there is an easy way of settling the question. We can dig up Shakespeare's skull, and compare the two. True, this may seem to offend against the letter of the epitaph

'BLESTE BE Y^E MAN Y^T SPARES THES STONES,
AND CVRST BE HE Y^T MOVES MY BONES.'

But there is no desecration in entrusting the noble remains of the poet to the enquiring eye of science; which will but learn something new from them, and place beyond doubt the value of another precious relic of him, and then restore them to the quiet of the grave."—(From the Tr. N. S. S., 1875–76. Appendix v.)

7.—Anonymous Article, in the *Birmingham Daily Post* of September 29, 1877, headed "General Grant at Stratford-upon-Avon," in the course of which Dr. Collis, the Vicar of the church there, is reported to have made some indignant remarks upon Mr. Parker Norris's article. "Having dilated upon the cool presumption of the author of the letter [article], Dr. Collis continued, that persons proposing such an experiment would have to walk over his prostrate body before they did it; adding that the writer even forgot to say, 'if you please.'" The American party, however, do not appear to have seen the matter from Mr. Collis's point of view.

8.—Anonymous Article, in the *Birmingham Town Crier* of November, 1877; a skit upon Mr. Collis's foolish speech. Beyond this censure, however, *nil de mortuo.* It is to be regretted that the worthy Vicar's remains were not buried in the church, so that persons approaching the grave with a laudable purpose might meet the reverend gentlemen's views, and "walk over his prostrate body."

9.—Shakespearian, A, in the *Birmingham Daily Post* of October 10, 1877, writes a sensible letter, taking Mr. Parker Norris's side of the question.

10.—Anonymous Article in the New York *Nation*, of May 21, 1878, in which we read: "Is it sacrilegious to ask whether it is wholly impossible to verify the supposition that the Stratford bust is from a death-mask? Would not the present age permit a tender and reverential scientific examination of the grave of Shakespeare?"

11.—Anonymous Article in the *Atlantic Monthly*, of June, 1878, in the section entitled "The Contributors' Club," where it is said—"Since the time seems to have come when a man's expression of his wishes with regard to what is to be done after his death is violently and persistently opposed by all who survive him, is it not a good opportunity to suggest that perhaps respect has been paid for a long enough time to the doggerel over Shakespeare's grave?

GOOD FRIEND FOR IESVS SAKE FORBEARE,
TO DIGG THE DVST ENCLOASED HEARE:
BLESTE BE Y^{E} MAN Y^{T} SPARES THES STONES,
AND CVRST BE HE Y^{T} MOVES MY BONES.*

* This is exactly as it stands upon the existing gravestone, not as it is reproduced by the writer in the *Atlantic Monthly*: the like as to the two lines of the epitaph in No. 6. The manuscript of Dowdall, referred to on p. 31 *ante*, is unfortunately modernized in *Traditionary Anecdotes*. He has, indeed 'friend,' and 'these,' as in the pamphlet version, but also 'digg,' and 'inclosed.' Dowdall, however, was a very inaccurate copyist. See fac-simile in Mr. J. O. Halliwell's Folio Shakespeare, vol. i, inserted between pp. 78 and 79. The Dowdall manuscript does not give the epitaph in capitals, except the initials.

When we consider how little we know of the great poet, and the possibility of finding something more by an examination of his tomb, it seems as if, with proper care, an investigation might be made that would possibly reward the trouble." The writer concludes thus—"Is it not advisable, then, to avoid waiting till it is too late? That is to say, unless, as I may fear, it is too late already."

12.—Warwickshire Man, A, in the *Argosy*, of Oct., 1879, in an article entitled, "How Shakespeare's Skull was Stolen." The *vraisemblance* of this narrative is amazing. But for the poverty of the concluding portion, which is totally out of keeping with the foregoing part, one might almost accept this as a narrative of fact.

13.—Gower, Ronald, in the *Antiquary*, of August, 1880, vol. ii, p. 63, "The Shakespeare Death-Mask," concludes thus—"But how, may it be asked, can proof ever be had that this mask is actually that of Shakespeare? Indeed it can never be proved unless such an impossibility should occur as that a jury of matrons should undertake to view the opened grave at Stratford; they at any rate would not need to fear the curse that is written above his grave—for it says, 'Cursed be *he* (and not *she*), who stirs that sacred dust.'" This is a 'new version' of the time-honoured line. I note too that Lord Ronald reproduces the "legal friend's" joke in Mr. Parker Norris's article. But I do not say he ever saw it.

14.—Halliwell-Phillipps, J. O., in his *Outlines of the Life of Shakespeare*, 1st edition, 1881, p. 86: 2nd edition, 1882, p. 172: 3rd edition, 1883, p. 233: writes thus—

"The nearest approach to an excavation into the grave of Shakespeare was made in the summer of the year 1796, in digging a vault in the immediate locality, when an opening appeared which was presumed to indicate the commencement of the site of the bard's remains. The most scrupulous care, however, was taken not to disturb the neighbouring earth in the slightest degree, the clerk having been placed there, until the brickwork of the adjoining vault was completed, to prevent any one making an examination. No relics whatever were visible through the small opening that thus presented itself, and as the poet was buried in the ground, not in a vault, the chancel earth, moreover, formerly absorbing a large degree of moisture, the great probability is that dust alone remains. This consideration may tend to discourage an irreverent opinion expressed by some, that it is due to the interests of science to unfold to the world the material abode which formerly held so great an intellect." Mr. Halliwell-Phillipps has more faith in the alleged precaution than I have. Surely a needy clerk, with an itching palm, would be no match for a relic-hunter. May we not here read between the lines, *q. d.*, 'to allow any one to make free with the masonry and explore the sacred dust?'

15.—Anonymous Article in the *Birmingham Daily Gazette*, of December 17, 1880, headed "Excavations in the Church and Churchyard of Stratford-upon-Avon." This repeats, on the authority of Washington Irving's *Sketch Book*, the story recorded by Mr. Halliwell-Phillipps. It is an alarmist article, censuring the Vicar's excavations, which were made indeed with a laudable purpose, but without the consent, or even the knowledge, of the Lay Impropriators of the Church.

16.—Anonymous Article in the Cincinnati *Commercial Gazette*, of May 26, 1883, headed "Shakspeare at Home," where it is said "Nor should they [the antiquarians of England] rest until they have explored Shakspeare's tomb. That this should be prevented by the doggerel engraved upon it, is unworthy of a scientific age. I have heard it suggested that if any documents were buried with Shakspeare, they would, by this time, have been destroyed by the moisture of the earth, but the grave is considerably above the level of the Avon, as I observed to-day, and even any traces connected with the form of the poet would be useful. His skull if still not turned to dust, should be preserved in the Royal College of Surgeons, as the apex of the climbing series of skeletons, from the microscopic to the divine."

17.—INGLEBY, C. M., *Shakespeare's Bones*, June, 1883, being the foregoing essay.

Printed by ROBERT BIRBECK, Birmingham.

www.ingramcontent.com/pod-product-compliance
Lightning Source LLC
Chambersburg PA
CBHW030719110426
42739CB00030B/995

* 9 7 8 3 7 4 4 6 7 7 8 3 7 *

Charles Ransley Green

Patriotic Lyndon
A History of Several Organizations at the County Seat of Osage County, Kansas

ISBN/EAN: 9783337306694

Printed in Europe, USA, Canada, Australia, Japan

Cover: Foto ©ninafisch / pixelio.de

More available books at **www.hansebooks.com**

PATRIOTIC LYNDON.

A HISTORY

Of Several Organizations at the County Seat of Osage County, Kansas the Last Seventeen Years, Which Have Made It a

"Patriotic Lyndon."

CONTAINING

The Roster of About 250 or More Ex-Union Soldiers and Sailors of the Late War, Who Have or Do Yet Gather at Lyndon for Decoration Days, With Their Post Office Addresses When Known, and In Cases of Death, Their Widows and Children.

TOGETHER WITH

The Roster and History of the Womans Relief Corps and Sons of Veterans. Sketches of the Commanders of Lyndon Post G. A. R., Prison Experiences, History of the Osage County Soldiers Battalion, Capt. Whinrey's Valley Brook Veteran Company, Capt. Joe Stavely's Lyndon Guards, History of Several Lyndon Band Organizations and List of Members.

Names of Those Whose Graves We Decorate in the Lyndon Cemetery, and Appendix for Corrections.

BY CHARLES R. GREEN,
Late a Member of the 101st O. V. I., Army of the Cumberland.
Member of the Kansas State Historical Society.

PRICE 35 CENTS.

LYNDON, KANS.
C. R. GREEN, PUBLISHER.

PREFACE.

Comrades and friends, the following 60 pages are drawn from my History or "Annals of Lyndon" and are offered to you by itself in pamphlet form at a price within reach of all, under the title of "Patriotic Lyndon," because, as you will see by the table of contents, it relates only to such organizations as have tended to build up patriotism to our country in Lyndon.

Valley Brook township and the country around was largely settled in an early day after the war by the old soldiers of our union. It has always been at the front in patriotism, and recognizing that the maintenance of these several organizations are conducive to the highest level of citizenship in our community, I have at infinite pains, spent all my spare time the last three months in examining records, copying rolls and interviewing older residents to get the matter in some shape to be printed. I have been as careful as possible, and so has my compositor; we have compared the notes and read proof repeatedly, but I am well aware how persistent figures and letters are in getting out of place in printing, and after the edition is printed there is only one remedy, and that is to make correction and put it in the appendix. Therefore, if you find a record wrong, look in the last of the book for corrections, and if not there, promptly notify me so that I can print the correction in the supplementary appendix and furnish it to you some months later.

I have introduced 13 war sketches of the Commanders of Lyndon Post, G. A. R., and Comrade Haas' prison story. They give one not familiar with war history a faint idea of what war meant during our four years of the Rebellion. The story of prison life down south where thousands of our noble soldier boys were deliberately starved to death or held in unhealthy prisons until diseases had planted their fatal seeds of death, can never be told.

The long weary months of life in our hospitals through the north, ended only by death, is the only record of tens of thousand who went forth in the morn of life to fight one enemy and were swept to the grave by a greater one —disease—is another story that cannot be told.

But there is a story that can be told, and for 32 years since the war the old soldiers have been telling it plainly that—"Treason was not right," and that those hot headed Southerners who tried to tear this union to pieces to build up slavery were whipped and that they surrendered with Genl. Robt. E. Lee to Genl. U. S. Grant at Appomattox, April 9, 1865, and that the Union-loving people of our land do not propose to let this government be run by those who tried to destroy it and the noble defenders of the union going down into beggars' graves.

Shall the service of 2,265,942 men (400,000 of which never lived to see the the close of the war) from our Northern land, engaged for four years and two months in 2,300 or more skirmishes, engagements and battles, every one of them at the cost of some one or more union life, be a useless sacrifice to our country's good? To the youth growing up in our homes I leave the answer.

Ever let us be a "Patriotic Lyndon."

C. R. GREEN,

Lyndon, Kansas, April 16, 1897.

INDEX.

COMMANDERS

LYNDON POST NO. 19, DEPT. KAN. G. A. R.

—:—

The Post was organized in 1880.

—:—

J. M. Whinrey, 1880-'81.
W. A. Cotterman, 1882.
John H. Howe, 1883-'87.
Sol Bowers, 1888.
George Weber, 1889.
John H. Howe, 1890.
Nels Hollingsworth, 1891.
D. H. Danhauer, 1892.
J. H. Buckman, 1893.
A. M. Sanderson, 1894.
C. R. Green, 1895.
D. F. Coon, 1896.
Wm. Rand, 1897.

PRESIDENTS

W. R. C. NO. 146, DEPT. OF KANS.

—:—

The Corps was organized February 2, 1887, and Mrs. Etta Howe installed the first President.

—:—

Mrs. Etta Howe, 3 years.
Mrs. Sophia Barnes, 1890.
Mrs. Martha Hollingsworth, 1891.
Mrs. Sarah E. Drew, 1892.
Mrs. Millie Weber, 1893.
Mrs. Anna Tomberlin, 1894.
Mrs. Lizzie Keenan, 1895.
Mrs. Mary Cotterman, 1896.
Mrs. Anna Olcott, 1897.

Indiana Soldiers.

2	Cav.	John W. Keenan, Co. E; a G. A. R.
40	Inft.	Nathaniel Y. Buck, 1st. Lieut. Co. B; a G. A. R.
137	"	H. B. Child, Co. H; a G. A. R.; died Aug. 17, 1892; buried at his home, Walton, Harvey county, Kan., where his family lives.
8	"	John Lefller, Co. A; a G. A. R.; removed to Muncie, Ind.
26	"	Israel N. Morris, Sergt. Co. K; living now at Quenemo, Kan.
83	"	Geo. W. Oard, Sergt. Co. F; died February 28, 1893.
84	"	Edward Shideler, Corp. Co. K; a G. A. R.
12	"	Austin M. Sanderson, Co. E; a G. A. R.
12	"	J. A. Sanderson, Co. E; a G. A. R.; moved back to Ind., 1895.
84	"	Amos L. Wilson, Co. K; a G. A. R.; lost a limb at Nashville.
84	"	L. T. Wilson, drummer Co. K; a G. A. R.
14	"	James Wells, Co. D, also in 13th Cav. Co. H; a G. A. R.
120	"	Geo. F. Burkdoll, Co. F; removed to southern Kansas.
30 145	" "	John H. Crowe, died March 28, 1882; his widow, Lydia A. Crowe removed to Kansas City, 1890.
84	"	Oscar Keenan, Co. B, also 57th Ind.; removed to Topeka.
42	"	Phillip Leffler, Co. B; removed to Royerton, Ind.
26	"	Warren W. Morris, Capt. Co. K; a G. A. R.; Washington, D. C.
51	"	A. W. Sargent, Co. I; removed to Anthony, Kansas.
132	"	Lew Sargent, Co. K; removed to Enid, Oklahoma.
42	"	B. F. Sloniker. Co. B; died February 12, 1894.
57 84	" "	Archibald H. Neff, Co's. E and K; now of Eaton, Indiana.
101	"	J. M. Carson, Co. A; a G. A. R.
72	"	Daniel Heron, Co. B; removed to Lane, Kansas.
26	"	Amos G. Morris, Co. K, removed to Ocheltree, Johnson Co., Kan.
83	"	Geo. W. Morris, Capt. Co. G, also 7 Vet. Reserve Corps, U. S. '64. Lives in Junction township. P. O., Vassar, Kansas.
47	"	Andy B. Wire, Co. H; removed to Indiana, 1896.
2	Cav.	W. B. Wright, Co. D; removed to Topeka in 1886.
25	Bat'y.	Frank A. Downs; removed East.
93	Inft,	Geo. W. Roberts, Co. E; removed some years ago.
16	"	Garret Voorhis, Co. D, dead; his widow, Mrs. Melinda Voorhis lived in Lyndon in 1890, has since removed.
12	Cav.	Jas. H. Asher, Co. A; removed to Greeley, Kansas.
54	Inf't.	Newton S. Wire, Sergt. Co. C; a G. A. R.
11	"	Rev. W. P. Elliott, Co. I, Gen. Lew Wallace's Zouave Regiment.
37	"	O. T. Hamlin, Co. G; Post-office, Vassar.

4 Cav. John Y. Urie, Capt. Co. F. Probate Judge from 1895—99.

84 " Phillip Wingate, died Dec. 12 1873. His father, James Wingate, lives at Albany, Delaware Co., Indiana.

OHIO SOLDIERS.

74 Inft David F. Coon, Co. H; a G. A. R.

187 " John M Barnes, Co. A; a G. A. R.

34 " John T. Andrews, Co. A; removed before 1890.

122 " D. H. Danhauer, Adjt. of Regt.; a G. A. R. Died March 14, 1896. The widow and daughter, Mrs. Wilbur Greene, and also son, Mr. H. Danhauer, live here.

196 " Joshua Evans, Co B; a G. A. R.

12 Cav. Nick Frankhouser, Co. I; Sheriff 1890-94. Removed to Osage City.

145 Inft. Horace L. Goodrich, Co. K; a G. A. R.

101 " Chas. R. Green, Co. A; a G. A. R

34 " }
36 " } Jerry Hussey, Co. D. Register of Deeds in 1988-92; removed to Lincoln twp., Williamsburg, P. O.

189 " John A Hooper, Co. G; removed to parts unknown.

151 " }
33 " } Abraham Primer, Co's. I and H; a G. A R.

58 " Ferdinand Ringhisen, Co, F.

156 " Noah Surface, Co. B; now of Junction twp, Vassar, P. O.

191 " John Starkey, Co. E; a G. A. R.

186 " M. C. Talyor, Co. G; removed to Paris, Ill. 1891.

39 " Thomas Williams, Co, G; a G. A R.

79 " J. M. Kirkbride, Co I.

136 " Simon Siples, Co. B; died Oct. 21, 1874. His widow Mrs. Siples, lives at Kansas City; Mrs. John Lord, a dau., lives with her mother.

54 " Martin Bannon, Co. K; died Jan. 12, 1874. Osgoods, of Quenemo, are relatives.

181 " Fred Sauers, Co. A; died Sept. 16 1877. His widow, Mary Jumper Sauers, married Mr. Stevens of Melvern.

192 " Wallace Green, Co. H; died May 16, 1887. His widow, Phebe Green, died 1895. There are four children living.

129 " A. W. Newton, Co. A; died Sept. 20, 1887. Amos Worral, Lyndon, is a friend.

15 " James P. Decker, 1st Lieut.; removed.

15 " }
46 " } Lyman W. Welch, Co's. H and E; removed to Horton, Kansas.

143 " John J. Robertson, Co. H; removed to Wooster, Ohio.

7 Cav. John C. Rankin, Co. E; Treas. of Osage Co., 1880-84; removed to Quenemo, Kansas; a G. A. R.

7 Inft. Geo. Thomas, Co. D; removed to Colorado Springs, Col.

26 " B. Albaugh, Co. A; removed to Osage City.

58 O. Inft. J. L. Clemence, Co. G; removed to Ohio, 1890.

49 " Jesse DeLong, removed to Florence, Kansas.

44 " } A. H. Criley, Co's. I and I; a G. A. . R
8 Cav. }

53 Inft. Sam'l J. McMurray, Co. A; removed to Nebraska.

140 " Wm. Rand, Co. C; a G. A. R.

156 " John B. McGaw, Co. A.

74 " Rev. D. M. Sleeth, Co. K.

IRREGULARS FROM OHIO:

E D. Atwell, in the Navy; removed to Burlingame, Kan. 1883 an old Roster gives him as Co. A, 178 O. V. I

T. E. Dempster, U. S. Navy, "Hudson," "Portsmouth," 32 months; died May 12, 1891, widow married Mr. Hobbs, 1895 now live at Pomona, Kansas. Daughter, Maud Dempster, lives at Lyndon.

F. A. Capper, Ist class fireman, U. S. Gunboat, "Naid", Marine Service; a G. A. R.

Wm. H. Jones B'v't. L't. Col., Additional Paymaster, U. S. A.

Illinois Soldiers.

73 Inft. Joseph H. Buckman, Co B; a G. A. R ; county cle k 1890-'92

36 " } Nathaniel G. Curry. Co.G, and also in Co K of the
114 Cav. } Cav. Reg , a G. A. R.

11 " Samuel Collins, Co. K; removed to St Joseph, Mo.

133 Inft. W. A, Cotterman, Co E; a G. A. R.

106 " John M. Fleming, Co D.

11 Cav. Robert S. Fleming, Co. C; died July 29, 1889; left a widow, Alvira A, Fleming, who died Nov. 4, 1895. Two children, O. A. and Cora. are living.

133 Inft. } Herbert Goodman. Co's. E and A; a farmer.
149 " }

52 " } Michael Hannigan, Co's. G and C; was working in the township in
65 " } April, 1889—has since removed to another place.

130 " } Wm Haas, Co's B and D; 13½ months a prisoner
77 " } Camp Tyler, Texas. Also in the 21st. Mo. S. M. a G.A. R.

130 " } James Henton, Co's. B and D; also a prisoner with Wm Haas at
77 " } Camp Tyler.

30 " John R. Henton, corporal, Co. B; a G. A. R.

92 " George S. Hawkins, Co. G.

33 Inft. Geo. W. Riggs, Co K; died Jan. 20, 1882. Widow died since; both are buried in the Dane Cemetery. Three children are living. Lewis, one of the children, lives with Andrew Peterson.

11 " Elijah Woodall, Sergt. Co I; a G. A. R.

123 Wilder's Mtd. Brigade, Elijah Hedges, Co C; a G. A. R. Removed to Charleston, Ill. 1891. P. O. now Fair Grove, Coles Co, Ill.

123 " Mtd. Inft., Francis McWhinney, Co. A; lost a limb in the war. Q. M. of Lyndon Post No. 19; a G. A. R.

123 " } M't'd. Inft., S. L. McWhinney, Co's. A and K; a G. A. R.
62 "

122 " J. Wm. Brooks, Co. H; died here 1873.

138 " Geo. W. Pryer, Co. B; died here 1874. Mrs. Tiffany is a sister.

15 " Saml R. Shoemaker; died Oct. 27, 1879. His widow md. J. T. Underwood, Florence, Kan.; Mrs. Florence Blackwell of Lyndon, is a daughter.

10 " Nels. Hollingsworth, Co. E; a G. A. R.

58 " Jas. A. McDonald, Sergt. Co. G; removed several years ago.

12 Cav. Chas. Manrose, Co's. L, E, and G; residing now at Osage City.

57 Inft. Isaac Morehead, Co. K; removed some years since.

42 " Francis Courtney, Co. D; died Feb. 16, 1880.

34 " John Pettigrew, Co. A; died June 17 1881. A son. Munroe Pettigrew, lives at Melvern.

123 " } M't'd. Inft., Elijah Williams, Co's. I and C; a G. A. R.
61 "

7 Cav. Dr. A. C. Tyler, Co. K; lived here until 1879, when he returned to Canton, Ill., where he died. His widow, Parmelia L. Tyler, lives here. Wm. Tyler, a son, is in U. S. Mail Service, Chicago, Ill.

30 Inft. J. T. Underwood, Co. B; removed to Florence, Kansas

36 " Dr. R. H. Chittenden, Co. H, also Hospital Steward, U. S. A.; now removed to Mound City, Holt Co, Mo; a G. A. R.

130 " S. H. Fuller, Sergt. Co. G; County Sheriff 1886-88; a G. A. R. Now lives at Carbondale, Kansas.

47 " Clark E. Henderson, Co. H; lives in Chicago. He is a son-in-law of M. Waddle, who lives here.

10 " Sidney S. McCurdy, Co. E; removed to Arkansas some years ago.

113 " Malcom F. Smith, Sergt. Maj., and Adjt. of the Regt.; 1st. Lieut. of Co. E; also in the 11th U. S. Inft. Adjt. of the Lyndon Post G. A. R., 1886. Removed to Ottawa and died there Feb. 10, 1896. Left a widow, and a son and daughter,

146 " Silas B. Tower, Co. A; Chaplain of the Lyndon Post G. A. R. One of Lyndon's early settlers. Died at the Soldiers' Home, Leavenworth, Kan., March 10, 1894; age 78.

20 Inft. J. Milton Whinrey, Capt. Co. F; in 36 battles commencing with Forts Henry and Done's n. Sheriff of th s county 1884–86: a G. A. R. Lives now at Passaic, Kearney Co. Kan.

15 " N. E. Wood, Co. I; former'y a G. A. R. here; removed to Ocalla, Florida, 1891.

130 " W. Hayes, Co. B; removed 1883, to place unknown.

10 Cav. F. J. Hyde, Co. C; removed 1883, to place unknown.

74 Inft. Horace W. Jenness, Co. G; also sutler of the Regt. Register of Deeds, Osage Co., 1880–84; now lives with his son, Fred Jenness, 1133 Monroe St., Topeka, Kansas.

63 " L. D. Burton, Co. D; removed 1884.

53 " J. B. Montgomery, Sergt. Co. B; removed.

73 " Alex. Pennington, died at Prairie City, 1879. The widow, Mrs Elizah P—., lived here 1883; now removed.

124 " David C. Cawood, Co. C; belonged to Lyndon G. A. R., 1890; removed East.

59 " } E. Ingersol', Co's. F and C; a broom maker in Lyndon, and a G. A.
89 " } R.–1890; removed.

85 " H. C. Swisher, Co. H. Sheriff 1892–96.

26 " Jacob Ward, Co. F; a G. A. R.

26 " Arthur Basel, Co. K; a G. A. R.

7 Cav. J. H. Harper, Co. F; now of Junction Twp., P. O., Vassar, Kansas.

78 Inft. George Painter, Co. I; who, with his wife reside with their son-in-law, Rev. Leigh. Mr. Painter, who is now 83, is the oldest member of the G. A. R. Post.

106 " C. S. Bellows, Co. A; moved here from Douglas Co. about 1894.

105 " H. Wakefield, Co. K; lived here in 1896, with his family, but now removed to his old home in Morris Co.

45 " Thomas M. Wallace, Co H; formerly a G. A R., here; removed to Salem, Fulton Co.. Ark., 1888.

Irregulars of Illinois service.

Elisha Oll'ott Sr., was in an Ill. Regt. of volunteers, 1832, during the Black Hawk war. He was an early settler here; died July 3rd., 1878. Ollcott Bros., Lyndon, are sons.

IOWA SOLDIERS.

4 Inft. Dr. Elbridge B. Fenn. Hospital Steward; died May 30, 1892. Widow, Mrs. E. W. Fenn, and daughter, Mrs. E. Waddle, live here. Geo. Fenn, a son, lives at Williamsburg, Kan.

2 Cav. Solomon Bower, Co. H; a G. A. R. Home here, residing temporarily at Salt Lake City, Utah.

10 Inft. Fred A. Downs, Co. A, also Commissary Sergt.; a G. A R.

16 " Charley A. Darling, Co. A.

9 " Rev. Eli F. Holland, Corp., Co. C; removed now to Mayetta, Kan.

7 Cav. Leeman Moore, Corp. Co. D; removed.

2 Inft. Joseph W Hammond, Co. C; removed in 1880, now in Oklahoma.

39 " Wm. Gibson, Co. E; died March 30, 1881. His widow, Maria Gibson and grown children, live near Quenemo, Kan.

2 Cav. John M. Arnold, Co. E; a G. A R Removed in 1890.

36 Inft. Rev. Geo W. Browning, Co. G; here in 1883, now at Council Grove, Kansas.

MASSACHUSETTS SOLDIERS.

5 Inft } John H. Howe (Mass.), Co's. I and F. Commander of Lyndon
13 " } Post G. A R. 6 years Col. of Osage Co. Batt'l. 4 years. Removed to his eastern home and died there June 24, 1894. His widow, Mrs. Etta Howe, who was President of the Lyndon W. R. C. for 3 years, now resides at Marlborough. Mass.

57 " Samuel H. Holyoke, Co. K; a G. A. R.

12 " N. H., Co. C, Geo. W. Harold, killed by a bull Aug. 31, 1885. His widow married John Tice.

NEW YORK SOLDIERS.

176 Inft. S. E. Shipman, Co. F; died in Oklahoma. Widow, Mrs. Maria Shipman lives here, also son Laverne and other children.

4 Art'y. Geo. W Doty, Co. H. Probate Judge 1889–91; a G. A. R.; removed to Burlingame.

4 Cav. Nathaniel D. Fairbanks, Q. M. Sergt., Co. K; a G. A. R. Died at Fort Worth, Texas, July 1st, 1892; family removed; dau. in N. Y

27 Inft. } John Foster (Fenn's cousin), Capt. Co. B; Lieut. Col., of the Reg..
28 " } a G. A. R.–removed.

1 Art'y. Charles E. Woodward, Co. D; a G. A. R.

6 Cav. J. J. Clark, Co. F; a G. A. R.

PENNSYLVANIA SOLDIERS.

211 Inft. David Findly, Corp., Co. I; removed prior to 1889.

135 " Rev. John P. Barber, Co. D; a G. A. R.; removed to Emporia, Kan.

9 Cav. } James R. Campbell, Co. H; Sergt. Co. F.
177 Inft. }

202 " Wm. H. Green, Co K; a G. A. R.

11 " James S. Kennedy, 1st. Lieut., Co. D.

11 " George Weber, Sergt. Co. D; a G. A. R.

105 " Fred Super, Co. C; a G. A. R. Removed to Pa.

David Uler, Co. K. Penn. Militia.

Michigan Soldiers.

11 Cav. Lewis A. Reynolds, Co. F; a G. A. R. Died June 21, 1893. A son is living.

10 " Harry Ford, Co. I.

6 Inft. } Walter Terrill, Co's. C and H; removed to Oklahoma.
1 Cav. }

1 Inft. Moses Terrill, Mich. Engineers, Co. F.

New Jersey Soldiers.

11 Inft. D. L. Hendershot, Co. E; a G. A. R. Removed to Bolivar, Mo., 1895

11 " David Lundy, Co. B, also Co. C, of the 12th N. J.; removed

Wisconsin Soldiers.

2 Cav. Wheeler Gilges, Co. F: a G. A. R. Removed to Lincoln twp., Rosemont, P. O.

17 Inft. W. J. Loose, Co. H; removed to southern Kansas.

Kentucky Soldiers.

37 Inft. Andrew J. Cox, Sergt. Co. G; removed to Mo., 1891.

1 Art'y. W. M. May, Batt'y E, 1st Ky. Light Art'y.

West Virginia Soldiers.

12 Inft. George Bane, Co. C; removed to Fairfax twp., Lyndon P. O.

15 " James Rogers, Co. I.

3 " } John Courtney Co. A; reinlisted in Co. F, 6th Cav. Died March 14,
6 Cav. } 1880; his widow, Josephine Courtney, and three children removed to Muncie, Indiana.

2 Cav. Henry Dunkle, Co. D.

1st and 2nd Neb. Cav., Aaron M. Buck, Co. G; a G. A. R.

Missouri Soldiers.

13 Inft. Patrick Dougherty, Co. H, also in the 5th Mo. Inft.; a G. A. R. Removed to Osage City; died there Feb. 27, 1893; buried in the Lyndon Cemetery.

5 Cav. } James A. Reading, Co's. I and G; a G. A. R.; removed to Lawrence;
13 Inft. } died there Oct. 14, 1895. He enlisted in Ill., but got put into a Mo. Regt. The widow, Mrs. Ellen Reading, and grown children, live in Lawrence, Kansas.

27 Jabez Adams, Co. L; a G. A. R. Supt. of Public Instruction, Osage Co., 1885–89. Removed to Lincoln twp., Rosemont. P. O.

32 John W. McIntire, Co. D; removed 1888.

9 Inft. Moses Bradford, Mo. State Militia.

1 " Robert H. Wynne, Sergt. Co. I; Mo. State Militia.

11 " John Gibson, Co. C. Mo. State Militia; removed.

21 " Leander Kimball, Co. K, Mo. State Militia; removed to Melvern, Kan.

Tennessee Soldiers.

2 Inft. James M. Kittrell, Co. A, E. Tenn., also Co. E 18 Ky. Inft.; a G. A. R. Been blind for many years.

4 " Ferdinand Singletary, 1st Lieut. of Co. B; died May 4, 1881. His widow, Mrs. Mary R. Singletary, remarried some years later to Oll. C. Deaver.

5 " John R. Poe, Co. C; a G. A. R. Removed to Hutchison, Kan.

Kansas Soldiers.

2 Inft. | Josiah R. Drew, Co. D, and Sergt. of Co. L; Kan. M't'd. Inft., 1st
11 " | Lieut. 18 U. S. C. T.; a G. A. R. Treas. of the Co. 1888–92; removed to Burlingame, 1892.

16 Cav. Benj. Tomberlin, Co. K; removed to Ottawa.

5 " John Wolf, Corp. Co. M; removed to Kansas City.

2 " Dr. J. A. Willey, removed to Mo.

15 " J. H. Rynerson, Co. G; died April 7, 1889. John Rynerson is a son, and Mrs. Frank Richards, a daughter.

13 Inft. Robert J. Wynne, Co. A; died Oct. 21, 1871. Widow, Nancy J. Wynne. lives with her dau. Mrs. Viola Smith, Helena, Montana.

13 " P. O. Roberts, Sergt. Co G; in 1890 removed to Nemaha Co., Kan, A dau. Mrs. J. McNichols, lives here.

11 " and Cav., John L. Bristow, Co. A.

11 " S. B. Enderton, Co. E. Register of Deeds of Osage Co. 1876–80; removed to Melvern.

Kansas State Militia.

23 " Dr. Geo. W. Miller, Co. D; called out in defence of Kansas, at the time of the Price Raid.

23 " W. A. Madaris, Price Raid. Kan. S. M.

23 " Elias A. Barrett, Q. M. of the Regt.; died July 5, 1880. Widow, Sarah F. Barrett, and son, Will Barrett. live here.

23 " Delos Watson, Price Raid Kan. S. M ; died June 16, 1887. Widow, Amanda Watson, lives in Lyndon, Mrs. J. H. Adams, Ottawa, Kan., is a dau. Two sons, E. O. and Dennis Watson, live here.

Colorado Soldiers.

2 Cav. Geo. E. Dorman, farrier, Co. M; removed 1894 to Lincoln twp. Waverly, P. O.; a G. A. R.

2 " } Olliver P. Rathburn, Co's. C and E; last known lived at Quenemo.
1 " }

5 " John H. Sowell, Sergt., Co. M; wounded in six places; now of Junction twp., Vassar, P. O.

SOME OF THE SOLDIERS WHO ARE (OR HAVE BEEN) MEMBERS OF THE LYNDON POST, BUT WHO LIVE OUTSIDE OF LYNDON AND VALLEY BROOK TOWNSHIP.

Arthur Basel, Co. K, 26 Ill. Inft.; Junction twp., Vassar.

August Storbeck, Co. G; 10 Minn. Inft. and 4 Minn. Batt'y., Vassar.

John Boyd, Co. C; 14 West Va. Inft., Vassar.

Wesley A. J. Maverty, Co. C; 132 Ind Inft., Vassar.

Capt. G. W. Morris, Co. G; 83 Ind. Inft., Vassar.

John H. Sowell, Co. M; 2nd Col., Cav., Vassar.

John A. Biand, Co. G; 2 Minn. Cav.; removed.

Cyrus L. Fix, Co. B; 9 Kan. Cav., Fairfax twp., Lyndon, P. O.

J. S. Rocky, Co. C; 105 Penn. Inft., Fairfax twp., Lyndon, P. O.

Geo. W. McMillin, Co. G; 70 Ind. Inft., Melvern.

Dr. W. C Sweezy, Surgeon, 140 Ind. Inft., Olivet.

L W. Powell, Co. G; 116 Ohio Inft., Olivet twp Osage City, P. O.

Chas. Cochran, Co. F; 12 Kan Inft., 1st Lieut. and acting Adjt. of the Regt Olivet.

S. B. Enderton, Co. E; 11 Kan. Inft., Melvern.

A. L. Lanning, Co. C; 122 Ill. Inft., Melvern.

R. R. Glass, Co. D; 13 Conn. Inft., removed to Melvern, thence in 1894, to Mammoth Springs, Ark.

Jacob aud Jonathan Hunt, privates of Co. G.; 10 Ohio Cav. They lived in Fairfax twp., were members of the Lyndon Post in 1889. I think they now live in Osage City.

Wilson B Henry, Co. F; 125 U. S. Colored Troop—3 years service on the Plains and in New Mexico 1865-68, Lyndon.

REMARKS.

B F. Sloniker, Co. B, 42 Ind. Inft; died at Quenemo, Feb. 12, 1894; buried in the Lyndon Cemetery. Widow, Mrs. Mary A. Sloniker, now lives with her son, Owen Sloniker, Eskridge, Kan.

Geo. W. Hufford, Co. E; 19 Ind Inft; lived in Fairfax twp; died March 15. 1888; buried at Mt. Zion Chapel. This was the first death in the Post, and the G A R. attended in a body, taking charge of the funeral. Will Hufford, a son, lives near Dragoon.

L R. Hale, Co I, 1 Minn. Inft.; died in Lyndon, buried at Melvern. The widow, Josie P. Hale, and children live in Lyndon. Mr. Hale told me that he belonged to a Batt'y. of Minn Inft. detached for service in the State against the Indians.

Corrections.

The numbers to the following names were disarranged in printing The mistakes occur at the top of page 104.

Geo. Thomas should be 57 O. V. I. instead of 7 O. V. I.

B. Albaugh, " " 126 " " of 26 "

J. L. Clemence, " " 18 " " of 58 "

Fred Super at foot of page 107, should be 100 Penn. instead of the 105 Penn.

On the first page of this Roster (page 101.), in the list of Commanders of Lyndon Post No. 19, J. M. Whinrey's name should have appeared as the first Commander of the Post. He served in 188 . Following this Roster is a History of the Post which was read at a Campfire Feb. 22, 1891. In this History, the first Commander is spoken of.

At the bottom of page 101 is an error; Jan., 1887 should read Jan., 1897.

THE WOMAN'S RELIEF CORPS.

NO. 146, DPT. OF KANSAS.

Lyndon, Kan.

The Corps was organized Feb. 2, 1887, and Mrs Etta Howe installed the first President.

Ninety five women have been connected with the order in the ten years of its existence, forty-six of which are now connected with the Corps. Two have died, many removed, and some dropped out.

Mrs. Margeret Arnold.
Mrs. Sophia Barnes.
Mrs. Elizabeth Buck.
Mrs. Francis Beasley.
Mi-s Lulu Barnes.
Mrs. Mary Bodenhammer.
Mrs Ellen Collins.
Mrs. Mary Colterman.
Mrs. Jcsie E. Cowan
Mrs Magg'e F. Chittenden.
Miss Agnes Childs.

Mrs. Amanda Downs.
Mrs. Sarah E. Drew.
Mrs. Ella Doty.
Mrs. Nora M. Downer.
Mrs. Laura Dorman.
Mrs. Susan Danhauer.
Miss Mary A. Green.
Mrs. Martha Greene.
Mrs. Emma Green.
Mrs Sarah E Gray.
Mrs. Annie Green.

Miss Lennie Grine.—Deceased.
Mrs. Nancy Fuller.
Mrs Lucy M. Foster.
Mrs. Emma Frankhouser.
Mrs Etta Howe.
Mis Martha T. Hollingsworth.
Mrs. Kate M. Holland.
Mrs. Emma Heaton.
Mrs. Hattie Heaton.
Mrs Emalira Hawkins.
Mrs Sarah A. Hoover.—Deceased.
Mrs. Dicie Hollingsworth.
Mrs. Sarah E. Hussey.
Mrs. Sarah C. Hunt.
Mrs. Mary Hand.
Mrs. Emma E. Holloway.
Mrs. Mary Hastings.
Mrs. Josie Hunting.
Mrs. Angie Huffman.
Mrs Johanna M. Hanson.
Mrs. Lizzie A. Keenan.
Mrs. Olive A. Leffler.
Miss Mary Leffler.
Mrs. J. W. Lord.
Mrs. Sarah McMillen.
Mrs. Alice Melick.
Mrs. Hettie E. Madaris.
Mrs. Lucy Manrose.
Mrs. Mary M McMillen.
Mrs. Mollie Newell.
Mrs. Anna Olcott.
Mrs. Louie W. Olcott.
Mrs. Ella Pleasant.
Mrs. Kate Pleasant.
Mrs. Lucy Potts.
Mrs. Emma D. Ransom.
Mrs. Kate A. Ringhisen.
Mrs. Emma Reed.
Mrs. Vera Rogers.
Miss Birdie Rogers.
Mrs. Lorinda C. Rand.
Mrs. Lurenda B. Smith.
Mrs. Margeret L. Sowell.
Mrs. Eliza J. Simmons.
Mrs. Mary A. Sloniker.
Miss Hattie B. Sweezey.
Mrs. Melinda Sweezey.
Mrs. A. M. Sanderson.
Mrs. Eliza Starkey.
Miss Jane Sanderson.
Mrs. Ada Smith.
Mrs. Parmelia L. Tyler.
Mrs. Carrie Trumbull.
Mrs. Margeret E. Taylor.
Mrs. Annie Tomberlin.
Mrs. Lucy Uber.
Mrs. Clara Wilson.
Mrs. Maggie Williamson.
Mrs. Mary I. Willett.
Mrs. Annie Widney.
Mrs. Millie Weber.
Miss Viola Wynne.
Mrs. Sarah Watson.
Mrs R. M. Wilson.
Mrs. Mattie F. Wheeler.
Mrs. E. Woodall.
Mis. Carrie M. Whitman.
Mrs. Minnie E. Whittemore.
Mrs. Miranda J. Wire.
Mrs. N. J. Wire.
Mrs. Mary A. Wire.
Mrs. Elanore Woodward.

Head Quarters Valley Brook Veteran Company,

Lyndon, Sept. 5, 1881.

Special Order No. 1

The members of this Co will meet at Lyndon Saturday, Sept. 10th at 2 P. M. for the purpose of drill and other business.

MILT WHINREY,
Capt. Com'dg Co.

The above notice I find in the Lyndon Leader (J. H. Stavely and H. H. Richardson editors) Sept. 8, 1881, and by further inspection of the same number learn that this Old Veteran Co. was well organized and officered as will be seen by the following list of the officers and non-commissioned officers, preparatory to its attending the state reunion at Topeka, Sept. 15, 1881.

THE LYNDON VETERAN COMPANY.

Officers and Non-commissioned Officers.

Milton Whinrey................Capt.
W. W. Morris..............1st Lieut.
D F. Coon.................2nd "
F. A. Downs..........Orderly Sergt.
S B. Tower.......Commissary "
J. H. Howe..........2nd Duty "
J. H. Courtney.......3rd " "
Geo. Weber..........4th " "
John Hinton.........5th " "
John H. Sowell.............1st Corp.
Wm. Hass.................2nd "
T. E. Dempster..............3rd "
F. Ringhisen...............4th "
Nels Hollingsworth........5th "

List of the company.

A. W. Sargent...Herbert Goodman
E. D. Atwell.........John Hooper
J. M. Barnes.....J. T. Underwood
Thomas Williams.....John Lefller
J. W. Keenan.........Lew Sargent
Joe Drew...........H. W. Jenness
R. H. Chittenden....P. Dougherty
John Wolf......Monroe Pettigrew
S. B. Endelton.......R. H. Wynne.
John C. Rankin.......J. A. Willey
W. A. Cutterman...J. H. Kennedy
Samuel Holyoke........A. B. Wire
L Kimball............Geo Herald
A. G. Morris ....Geo. Hufford
G. S. Hawkins.....G. W. Browning
W. C. Sweezey.......Chas. Cochran
I. N. Morris............E. Woodall
N. D. Fairbanks......B G. Wilson
Geo. W. Riggs...S. L. McWhinney
D H. Danhauer........R. R. Glass

The regiments of the above soldiers show in other places in this roster.

G. L. Geoffrey, Corp. Co. D; 12 Kan. Inft
Daniel Heron, pri. Co. B; 75 Ind. Inft.
Anderson Hunt, " Co. K; 122 O. V. I.
H. H. McKane, Corp. 91 O. V. I.
James Ackley, pri. Co. K; 8 Kan. Inft.
John Burgess, " Co. C; 27 Mich. "
Wm. Wise, Sergt. Co. F; 47 Ind. "
P. F. Wellman, Surg. U. S. A.
J. G. Marshall, pri. Co. B; 56 Pa. "
J. G. Ellis, pri. Co. G; 74 Ill. Inft.
G. W. Metzler, pri. Co. A; 120 O. V. I.
E A. Richards, pri. Co. D; 5 Kan. Cav.
G H Blair, pri. F; 1, O. Light Art'y.
Robert Neil, Sergt. Co. I; 5 W. Va. Inft.
B. E. Tweed, Sergt. Co. B; 172 O. N. G.
Levi Shrader, pri. Co. B; 17 Kan. Inft.
James Thompson, pri. Co. C; 1 Ia. Cav.
A. J. Utley, Provost Marshall.
Henry Howell, Sergt. Co. C; 14 W. Va. I.
Wm. King, pri. Co. D; Mo. Guard.

Note. At a Camp Fire held April 6, 1891, in the Opera house to celebrate the Silver Anniversary of the Grand Army Order. The following sketch was prepared and read at the request of the Post by C. R. Green, Historian.

ORGANIZATION AND HISTORY
OF
LYNDON POST, NO. 19.
DPT. OF KAN., G. A. R.

Steps to permanently organize Lyndon Post, No. 19, Dpt, of Kansas, were taken by Comrades resident here, early in the year 1880.

March 27, J. T Underwood, now residing at Florence, Kan., having received the proper books and authority, called a meeting and J. M. Whinrey was elected the first Post Commander.

The following is the list of the Charter members. J. M. Whinrey, Jas. Kennedy, Wm Harris, J. T. Underwood, F. A. Downs, John Sowell, Andy B. Wine, J. W. Hammond, H. H. Murray and W. A. Cotterman.

We are indebted to Comrade Downs for a complete record of these first meetings, as he was chosen by Comrade Whinrey to serve as the first Adjutant.

The place of meeting in these days was the Averill Hall over D. F. Coon's Clothing Store; they afterward met in a hall over Horace Clark's Hardware Store; in 1885, they were able to occupy the present G. A. R. Hall in Mr. Howe's building.

There seems to have been a hitch somewhere in the growth of the order in the earlier years of its history in this place; not until 1882, did the boys seem to become thoroughly interested. Not being a member then, I will ascribe all hindrances to a Kansas drougth. But in 1882 and '83 we had a bountiful harvest; twenty six joined in '82, and twenty-seven in '83. Since that time the old Boys have from far and near connected themselves with the Post, until our books show one hundred and eighteen names with about one half that number in active connection with the Post at this time. Justice should however be granted to a large number in our midst, who, though not paying members, come very promptly to our aid in the times of work, and upon public occasions when it is desirable that all the Boys in blue should fall in line.

There are about one-hundred old Soldiers residing in the township, but we have members in Olivet, Malvern, Agency, Junction and Fairfax townships, who gather with us at different times during the year.

While we decorate twenty-six old Soldiers' graves in our Lyndon and Valley Brook Cemeteries, this Post, strictly speaking, has never buried but one of its own members, viz., Geo, Hufford. We have, however, assisted in the burial of a good many old Boys, and we are grateful to the Heavenly Father who has spared our lives and supplied our wants thus far on this march of life; and when we, too, hear that final bugle call to cross the Jordan, may the rising youth be ready to take up our mantles.

Comrades and Friends, you have been familiar during all these eleven years with the workings of our Post.

It has placed no small part in public doings here. We have helped you to celebrate our National anniversaries of Independence. We have twice pitched our old Soldiers' Reunion Camp beside the village. We have striven to care for the sick and afflicted among our soldier friends. Decoration Day has never passed without a proper observance of its spirit, and how often has the day drawn friends together from all over the country to strew flowers o'er the graves of their departed. We, as a Post, labored in your midst to inaugurate the movement which culminated in our Auxiliary, The Woman's Relief Corps, now such a popular and useful order among our wives and daughters. We have all along during these years given you treats, in Camp Fires and G. A. R. sociables; and, it would be unnecessary for me to further enumerate our work. But amid all these years the fact must not be forgotten that a Post to be successful, must have devoted, energetic officers. The finances must be kept up, the proper books and reports made out and over and above all, the Commander must keep a vigilant eye. This order has no salaried office. Fraternity, Charity, and Loyalty, is our motto, and no one labors in vain for the possession of these virtues.

Commander J. M. Whinrey was followed by W. A. Cotterman as Commander. J. H. Howe was the next successor and he was continued in office four successive years. Sol Bower served one term and was succeeded by Howe, who served one term, going out of office last Jan. in favor of the present incumbent, Comrade Hollingsworth. Such in brief are the essential features of our Post History. How few now days realize that it is twenty-six years since the close of the war, and that not until several years after, that was the city of Lyndon founded, and that only a few more years, and this place will know us no more. Then Comrades and Friends, lend us a kindly hand as we endeavor to keep up this order in our declining years.

W. A. Cotterman.

Andy Cotterman was born at Loami, Sangamon Co, Ill, Dec. 10, 1817. He enlisted May 2, 1864, as private in Co. E 133 Ill, National Guards. The Regt. was sent to Rock Island where they guarded Rebel prisoners the summer of 1864. He was mustered out Sept. 24, 1864. Re-inlisted in the 149 Ill. Infr., but was thrown out for physical disability.

He came to Kansas June, 1870, settling with his father and sister at Lyndon. Removed to Osage City Oct., 1871. Here he filled the office of deputy post master three years—1873 to 1876. He was elected Clerk of the Dist. Court 1878, which office he held 6 years. He married Mrs. Mary Payne Jan. 7, 1879, and again settled down in Lyndon. They have two children, Eugene and Judith Cotterman. From the first, he has been one of the proprietors of the Cotterman-Wilson Grain and Elevator Co. They commenced it Nov., 1889 and had it ready to receive grain by Feb. 4, 1890, Monroe Stivison unloading the first load of corn that day.

W. A. Cotterman was the 2nd Commander of Lyndon Post, 1882. Always active in politics, alive to Lyndon's best interest, he needs no further notice from my pen to commend him to future historians.

Short sketches of the Commanders of the Lyndon Post.

Sol Bower, Fourth Commander of Lyndon Post—1888.

Solomon Bower was born in Summit county, Ohio, November 7, 1832. His father died there in 1841, and when Sol was twelve years old his mother, with her family of four children, removed to Joliet, Ill. In March, 1857, when 25 years old, he went to Kansas and espoused Freedom's cause. He once said in a letter to me, that as a youth he had very deep feelings on these matters. He had been taught the evils of slavery and could not stand idly by and see Kansas made a slave state and not take a hand in the fight. So early in the season of 1857 he came to Lawrence, and made that his home.

Early in the year of 1861 he went to Iowa to visit a brother. While there Fort Sumpter was fired on and he enlisted, June, 1861. in Co. H., 2nd Iowa Cav. He did service in this until May, 1863, when he received an honorable discharge for physical disability, and returned to Lawrence, Kansas, where he was living with his mother when, on August 21, 1863. o d Quantrell and his gang of murderers made their raid on Lawrence. shooting down in cold blood about 200 persons, of which 113 died and 30 were desperately wounded. Seventy-five stores, hotels, and business houses were burned, and nearly one hundred dwellings. Two million dollars' worth of property was destroyed in the four hours that they had possession of Lawrence; 80 widows and 250 orphans were left behind.

"We lived just outside of the city corporation near where the guerrillas entered the city. Our house was the first one attacked. Snider, living in the same house with us, was the first man killed in the raid, and I was their second mark, but nine shots at short range proved me to be bullet-proof, so they let me off. Later in the raid a brother was killed in the city. They came early in the morning, three or four hundred strong, and Lawrence had no soldiers to guard it, nor any warning of the proposed raid, and had it not been for their great haste to get on into the city before the people were aroused we would have suffered more.

"I was married in Lawrence Nov. 5, 1865 to Miss Julia A. Thornton. She came from Athens county, Ohio to care for a brother who had received five wounds in the Quantrell raid at Lawrence.

"In these early years after the war Lawrence was quite a place for the headquarters of various Indian agents, traders, etc., who were connected with the tribes living in Franklin and Osage counties. Anticipating the treaty with the Sac and Fox Indians and final occupation of these lands, some prominent monied men of Lawrence selected me as an advance guard, to go down to the Sac and Fox agency in the spring of 1867, to look out for their interests. Their design was, upon the ratification of the the treaty by Congress, throwing open the Indian reserve for settlement, to have a town site secured in the section around where Lyndon was some years later located, that could be made a railroad metropolis and county seat. We secured permission from the Indian agent to locate at the Agency, and opened out a hotel, but this did not suit us, and after waiting two years for the diminished reserve to be thrown open lawfully, in the fall of 1869 I went up beyond Olivet on the "Trust Lands" and bought a quarter section of land of a man by the name of Hammon; we, however, received our deed from Bob Stephens. I went right to work building me a house, and before the spring election of 1870 we were once more living in a home of our own.

"I was so busy then that I paid little or no attention to election or township matters. Arvonia then embraced all the southwest quarter of Osage county, 12 by 15 miles, and there were no improvements then from the Agency to Olivet, which was a mile east of my place and only a few families there. West of me, I remember none until we got to Jim Jessee's. For some time we did our principal trading at Lawrence, later, in Osage City. At first it was very lonesome to us, but neighbors gradually came in and we enjoyed farm life.

"Before going on to speak of township affairs I wish to go back a year or two and give a little history of the advent of settlers on the Indian Reserve: While living at the Agency watching the movements of the Indians and Congress, I found plenty of others equally as vigilant, though not as well posted. Albert Wiley had been confirmed Indian agent in March, 1867, and by October, 1868 certain parties had negotiated a treaty with the Sac and Fox Indians, that, when confirmed by Congress, would extinguish their claim to the Diminished Reserve and throw open many thousand acres of the finest lands in Kansas for settlement by anyone who, being first occupant of the claim, should pay the price of one dollar and fifty cents per acre. Before the treaty was made there were many persons all over the Reserve selecting claims, thinking they could hold them after the treaty was ratified. But the Indians laid in a complaint and the Government sent soldiers to clear the Reserve of all whites except those who had permission from the Agent to stay. As soon as the treaty was made, and before it was ratified, the Reserve was filled again with claim hunters, and again the U. S. troops were called on to drive them off. Many of the home seekers camped on lands adjacent to the Reserve and organized to protect and stand by each other. And thus through a long siege of dread, worry and fear, finally gained possession of their claims.

"With this lengthy digression I will now return to my new home. As I said before, I was very busy with my affairs around home in April, 1870 when one day an oldish sort of a man rode up and inquired if I was Mr. Bowers; introducing himself as John Perrill. He said that he lived nine miles west of my place, and at the recent township election had been elected road overseer in his road district, and as he had an important road matter to look after at once he desired me to duly qualify him into his office. I was very much astonished at the latter part of his conversation, and told him that I was no public officer to swear folks into office, and that he had come to the wrong place. He replied that I had been legally elected trustee of Arvonia township, and wanted to know if I hadn't had my legal notice of said election. I told him his notice was the first information I had had of it. "Well," said he, "it is correct, and as I live so far away and cannot come again, and the exigencies of the situation demand my being installed into my office at once, I will ask you to fill out and sign my papers and save me another trip.' I stood out about doing such act until I had authority, but he begged so piteously that at last I yielded, made out his papers, administered the oath and started him away a full fledged official.

"I did not care to have this known very much in those days, but John Marsden, the trustee of Melvern township, and I used to talk over our official cares occasionally together, and we always had a big laugh over this.

"I was elected trustee again in Arvonia in 1871. September 4th the county commissioners created Olivet township out of Arvonia and Agency, and I resigned my office in Arvonia only to be appointed trustee in my new township of Olivet, and was elected in succeeding years to the same office.

"In 1876 I ran against E. H. Marcy in the 61st District as Republican nominee for Representative to the State Legislature, and at the election November 7th received 1,001 votes to his 358. Again two years later, I ran for the same office against H. Kirby, Greenbacker, and James M. Wood, Prohibitionist, beating Kirby by 33 votes. D. H. Danhauer was my colleague from the 60th District in this county both terms. I lived in Olivet until 1885. I served as trustee 7 terms, township treasurer two terms, school district treasurer 9 terms and member of the Legislature two terms. I wound up my public life by serving two years as mayor of the city of Lyndon.

"After a few years on our Olivet farm where stock and farming paid reasonably well, I had to quit it on account of physical infirmities. We had a pleasant neighborhood and enjoyable time there. As I said before, we moved to Lyndon in 1885. During our long residence in Kansas we can credit much the largest share on the sunny side of life. This has already grown too lengthy, so I will stop.

Sol Bower.

——o——

D. H. DANHAUER.

David H. Danhauer was born in Muskingum county, Ohio, January 7, 1837. At the age of ten years he was left an orphan in the world, the youngest of eight children. He had a good common school education and learned the trade of a shoemaker.

March 2, 1854 he married Susan F. Groves of Taylorsville, Muskingum county, Ohio. They settled in Deaverstown, but after four years removed to Duncan Falls, Ohio, which was their home until they removed to Kansas.

Three children were born to them before the war—Henry G., Willie S., who died aged three, and Louis H. The last only a month old baby when Mr. Danhauer went off to the war.

He enlisted as a private in Captain Peache's company—Co. A, 122 Ohio Volunteer Infantry, August 19, 1862. Capt. Peach raised this company in and around Mr. Danhauer's town, and although Mr. D. was only twenty-five years old, he was considered to be one of the older ones and was at once elected to the place of first sergeant.

Early in his war service, at Parkersburg, Va., he was afflicted with the sickness that was with him all his after life, and finally resulted in his death. But he did not leave the regiment. In fact he never was absent from it during the war, so far as Mrs Danhauer knows, except when home on furlough near the close—Feb., 1865.

March 4, 1864 he was promoted to First Lieutenant, and made Adjutant of the regiment. He was in Gen. Milroy's Division, 6th Corps, Army of the Potomac.

He was in battles and campaigns as follows: 1862, Winchester, Va.; 1863, Nov. 8, Brandy Station, Va ; 1864, all through that terrible Wilderness fight, where, May 5, 6 and 7, and at Spottsylvania 8th to the 14th Grant lost 64,178 killed, wounded and missing; Cold Harbor, June 1st to 15th; Bermuda Hundred; finally getting on to the left at Petersburg, June 22, '64.

July 4, 1864 their division was transferred to the Army of the Shenandoah under Genl. P. H. Sheridan, where Mr. Danhauer's regiment had a hand in the battle of Opequan, Sept 19, 1864, Fishers Hill, Mount Jackson, New Market, and last the sudden surprise made on the union army by Gen. Early at Cedar Creek, October 19th; their sudden retreat and Sheridan's "twenty mile ride' to save the day, all ending in glorious victory.

Then there was a little affair at Kernstown, Nov. 12th, which ended their service in the Shenandoah valley. In February, 1865 their division was sent back to Grant's army in front of Petersburg. March 25th they broke lines and rested no more until two weeks later when old Lee surrendered at Appomattox, April 9th. General Wright commanded the 6th corps then. Immediately after Lee's surrender Comrade Danhauer's corps was ordered southward to assist Sherman's army in capturing Genl. Joe Johnson's rebel army in the Carolinas. But before they got there he surrendered and went home with the rest.

May 23rd and 24th the armies under Genls. Grant and Sherman passed in Grand Review previous to discharge.

They were mustered out there June 26, 1865, and soon after discharged and paid off at Columbus, Ohio.

When he returned home from the war he went into the dry goods business there at Duncan Falls, but not liking it, in a year or two he went back into his old boot and shoe trade, selling eastern stock and making home-made goods for all who desired.

In the fall of 1870, having sold out their home with a purpose of buying one with more land attached, so that their boys could follow farming, Mr. Danhauer, after receiving some Kansas papers from a Mr. Millner here at Lyndon, was led to come west and look around. He liked it so well here that he bought a farm 3 miles north of Lyndon that they still own, and that Henry Danhauer lives on, and also bought several town lots in Lyndon. He went back to Ohio and stayed there that winter. In the spring Atwells, Deavers and themselves came on, arriving at Lyndon March 30, 1871, settling on their farm at once. Their family then consisted of five—the two boys above spoken of, born before the war, and Annie D, who was about two and a half years old when they moved here, and the parents. Nora D. was born after they had settled here. three and a half years.

They lived on their farm nine years. In common with others they stayed right here through all the grasshopper drouthy years and know what privations a settler has to endure in a new country. Mr. D. worked at his shoemakers' bench on the farm and one year, after Mr. Hancock, a shoemaker in Lyndon died, he bought out his stock, occupied his old shop and worked here a year, going back and forth from the farm.

Mr. Danhauer was elected to the Legislature two terms—Nov. 7, 1876, for two years from January, 1877, and another two years' term in 1879.

They moved into Lyndon October, 1881. Henry had been married to one of Elijah Woodall's daughters a year or so and he went onto the farm. Mr.

Danhauer moved into the Dr. Fenn residence, where they lived six years Mr. D. bought into the grocery store in the brick front building with Findley Robinson. He became owner of the building afterward, selling out his stock to Gutwillig; and the building in time passed into Clarence Martin's and Horace Clark's hands. Mr Danhauer also followed merchandising in Findley Robinson's new stone building on the opposite side of the street, which they sold out to Oneal Bros.

When Mr Danhauer sold out his brick front store to Clarence Martin he moved back on to his farm, where he stayed until February, 1889, or about two years. Then from increasing infirmities he felt that he must give up farming, so the farm was rented out and he returned to Lyndon. This time they lived in the Whinrey house, which Mr. R. B. Vail now owns and occupies, one year, and then bought out Mr. Simmons' residence in block 40, where they have since resided.

It was 1890, the second year in town, that he served as Commander, and performed such other duties as his fellow citizens laid upon him. It was their intentions, as soon as out of debt to once more go back and visit their old Ohio home. Mr Danhauer said to his wife that the mortgages were paid last year and this year (1897) was to have been the year for their contemplated trip, but the Lord willed otherwise.

March 14, 1896 Mr. Danhauer died and the widow does not care to go back now

Henry Danhauer married Ida F. Woodall in 1880 and has five children. They live on the farm.

Lew Danhauer, with his boy H. Wallace Danhauer, lives in San Francisco, California.

Annie Danhauer married Wilbur Greene of Lyndon and lives with the mother. Her husband following mercantile business or such other employment as these stringent times gives one. They have two little girls.

Nora E Danhauer married Harper C. Murphy of Sedalia, Missouri in 1896, and both follow teaching in the commercial college there at Sedalia.

DECORATION DAY AT LYNDON—1884.

This was a red letter day for the old soldiers around Lyndon. This is not to be a review of the day; full accounts can be read in the Lyndon papers of that date. The Post turned out in full force, well uniformed. The procession from the city to the cemetery was about a mile long of teams. After the decoration services were over, Harry Ford took four pictures, that at this late day have a historic interest.

1st. A picture of the Flower Girls, Band, old soldiers and others out in the cemetery. And second a picture of the Flower Girls in their conveyance.

—

NAMES OF THE FLOWER GIRLS.

Lucy Williams,	Cora Woodall,
Carrie Hedges,	Winnie Green,
Elva Buck,	Emma Kennedy,
Anna Kennedy,	Ida McWhinney,
Alice Hawkins,	Emma Hinton,
Effie Courtney,	Myrtle Wolf,
Mary Williamson,	May West,
Mamie Ayers,	Vesta Geyer,
Lucy Underwood,	Nora Danhauer,
Addie Drew,	Edith Hollingsw'th
Mamie Keenan,	Lulu Barnes,
Lilie Leller,	Grace Cottrel',
Nellie Fleming,	Ada Glass,
Emma Heaton,	Lula Peairs,
Celia Black,	Dollie Whittemore;
Luna Gardner,	Ettie Gardner,
May Trumbull,	Cora Fleming,
Flo Madaris,	Flora Shenaker.

SKETCHES OF THE LIVES OF J. M WHINREY AND JOHN H. HOWE, FIRST AND THIRD COMMANDERS OF LYNDON POST.

J. Milton Whinrey was the first Commander of the Post.

He was born in Clinton Co., Ohio July 23, 1840. Lived in Cass Co, Mich., and Joliet, Ill.; here he enlisted April, 21, 1861 in the 3 months service, after the firing on Fort Sumpter. They did not leave the state. June 21, 1861, they were mustered into the U. S. service. He went as a private in Co. F, 20, Ill. Inft. In 1864 he veteraned with the Regt, and while home then on a furlough in Ohio, he married Miss Emily Lieurance, April 14, 1864. He was in 36 battles commenceing with Forts Henry and Donelson, and Shiloh. He was in the 17th Corps, Army of Tennesee. He saw over four years service and came out Capt. of his Company.

After the war, in the fall of 1873, he moved into Osage Co., Kansas, buying the 80 from the same quarter in which Rev. Green of Junction twp., lives. He only farmed there one year, after which he returned to Ohio, and stayed two years.

In the spring of 1876, he moved back sold his 80 for stock and lived on rented farms until the year of 1882, when he bought the Capper farm one mile east of Lyndon, paying $2,800 for it. Two years later, being elected to the office of County Sheriff, he sold his farm to H C. Cates for $5,500, and moved into town.

In these years of 1876 and '82, Milt Whinrey was known all over the country as a very successful Auctioneer at public sales.

The next several years were very disastrous ones to him. As he had used considerable of his means in building himself a home, and also expended somewhat for his re-election, he was hardly prepared for the defeat he received in not being re-elected. The death of his wife, and depreciation of Lyndon property broke him up, and he went out to Kearney Co., Kansas and homesteaded. Some time afterward he married Miss Livonia Pryer of Lyndon, who had a claim near him. His childrens' names are—Norah E. Whinrey, married to Eugene Bailey of Lyndon; Estelle I. W—., who died at the age of 11 at Lyndon; Olive P. W—., who is about 18; she, together with the youngest child, Myrtle Ethel W—., born 1882 on the Capper farm, live at their home in Passaic, Kearney Co., Kan.

Comrade Whinrey and wife visited the Osage Co. friends the fall of '96 and they were made to feel that this is yet a good section of country to live in; and when fortune permits, we will welcome them back to Lyndon.

——o——

DECORATION DAY—1884.

Floral Committee.

Mrs. Etta Howe,	Mrs. J. H. Keenan,
Mrs John Hinton,	Mrs. P. Lefler,
Misses,	Misses,
Flora Keenan,	Cora Shoemaker,
Ella Lefler,	Gusta Kercher,
Dora Waddell,	Belle Uber,
Clara Beaver,	Ida Smell,
Ella Carey,	Anna Brown,
Mary Green,	Maggie Kennedy,

Grace Morris.

"Bring all the flowers you can and deliver at the office of Dr. Chittenden"

J. H. HOWE,

Commander 1883-87.

John Hale Howe was born in Berlin Mass., May 13. 1838. He removed to Marlborough at the age of 18 and worked at the shoemaker's trade until he enlisted and went to the war.

June 29, 1861, he enlisted in Co. F 13, Mass. In one mouth their Regt. was on its way to the Potomac. Their first service was in the Upper Potomac army around Harper's Ferry, Sharpsburg, Darnstown, and Williamsburg.

He was on provost guard duty seven weeks at Hagerstown, Md. Dec. '61 and Jan. '62. March 1, 1862 they crossed the Potomac into Martinsburg. Va. They formed part of Gen. Banks and Gen. Shields army to occupy Winchester and Bunker Hill, Va. Some skirmishing was had with the rebels under Jackson; after this movement, in March, 1862 they werr ordered down to join Gen. McDowel at Centerville.

One of the singular freaks of war is that they broke camp and left it three different days and each night found them back in the same vicinity so that they camped on the same grouad three nights in succession.

They moved to Bull Run, to Manasses Junction, and the 12th of May 1862, to Falmouth, under Gen. Hartsworth. The marching and counter-marching was so fatiguing that Comrade Howe got detailed to drive a team, but as the army fell back on Washington he gave out entirely and went to a hospital in Washington. July 4th he joined his Regt. at Warrenton Centre, C. H., but being unable for duty, was given an honorable discharge July 18. 1862 and sent home to Mass.

Here, May 3, 1863 he married Miss Etta Dole at Berlin, Mass.; but July, 1864, feeling his country's call for more help, he enlisted in Co. I 5th Mass. He served one-hundred and sixteen days as a guard at Baltimore; receiving an honorable discharge Nov. 16, 1864, he again returned home; this time for good.

J. H. Howe and wife came to Osage Co., May, 1868 Sam Holyokes were fellow townsmen of theirs in Mass. and they stopped here with them until the fall of 1868, when they were able to occupy, peaceably, a claim on the Salt Creek bottoms. one half mile south of where Lyndon was established in 1869.

In Mrs. Etta Howe's narrative, which is given in another place, some of the early day trials of these pioneers is given along with others.

From the first organizition of the G. A. R. in Kansas. he was interested; and, although absent in Mass with his wife, for a peiod of five years during the '70's, he retained his farm. When he returned, he engaged in the sale of agaicultural tools; hauling them down to his farm from Burlingame, where the settlers came and dealt liberally with him.

On the organization of the Lyndon Post No. 19, in 1880, we find him on hand; and in 1883 he was elected Post Commander. December 1881 he removed from his farm to town, where he opened an agricultural tool store, buying for that purpose the old H. Gilbert property in block 27. This made him a good residence anb store combined.

Mrs. Etta Howe personally assisted him in his business and became acquainted with his customers. They were both very enthusiastic in the Grand Army work, and, during the six years from 1882, helped to increase the Post from thirty six to over one hundred members, and in 1887 Mrs. Howe and other Lyndon ladies instituted the

Woman's Relief Corps. Mr. Howe's business having increased, in 1884 he bought a large building (Deaver's carriage shop) and moved it onto his premises. It was in the second story of this building that he finished off the nice large hall, which the Grand Army and Woman's Relief Corps occupied so many years.

Space will not admit of further mention of his care and devotion to the old soldier's interest in Lyndon "The old boys" will always carry his love for them, in pleasant remembrance. In his dying hours he sent his last message to them.

August 31. 1882, when they were building the new Methodist church, there was a mass meeting in its yard of old soldiers and citizens of Osage County to listen to a speech from Senator Preston B. Plumb. This was addressed particularly to the old soldiers; and, at the close of the day there was a re-organization and re-election of the officers of the Osage County Battalion.

This was an organization composed largely of the Grand Army Posts of Osage County: and, probably not a half dozen other counties in the state were as well organized as this county. Comrade J. H. Burke was elected Colonel of our Battalion on this occasion. I do not remember who was elected Colonel in 1883, but Comrade Howe was elected Lieut. Colonel, and in 1884 he was elected Colonel; likewise in '85 and '88. One of these years D. H. Danhauer was his Adjutant.

In the fall of 1884, a very successful reunion was held in the eastern part of the city of Lyndon. Some three or four hundred old soldiers being present and plenty of tents set up to make a large camp. Commander Howe and Lyndon Post had plenty of work to do. They afterwards had the satisfaction of knowing that it was a social success

Comrade Howe's large acquaintance with the old soldiers and others in the county, was, I think, the means of some of them abusing his confidence in succeeding years, to the extent of many hundred dollars. Because of so many not paying for their tools, buggies. etc., Comrade Howe was obliged to make an assignment.

He held city offices and filled places of trust, and when from long continued ill health, he went East to live and die, one of the largest orders in Lyndon, The Modern Woodman of America, April 1893, passed resolutions of regret, and expreessd many hearty wishes as to his future health, hapbiness, and prosperity. Many kind letters passed back and forth from the Post and Corps here, to Mr. and Mrs. Howe in their home at Marlboro, Mass., prior to Mr. Howe's death, which took place June 24. 1894. As our Lyndon papers contained full account of his passing away at the time of it, the task of the historian will close with a prayer that the widow may find as warm friends in the East as they left behind them here in the West.

GEORGE WEBER.

Comrade George Weber, the seventh Commander of Lyndon Post No. 19, was born near Harmony, Butler county, Pennsylvania, January 7, 1839.

This was always his home until he removed to Kansas in 1867.

WAR HISTORY.

(Given in his language.)

"I enlisted April 23, 1861, in Co. D. 11 Pa. Reserves. We did not leave the state at once. Gov. Curtin raised 13 regiments of Inft., 1 of Cav., and one of Art., called the Pennsylvania Reserves, numbering 15,000 men. The first battle of Bull Run occurred July 21, 1861 and our Pa. Reserves were ordered at once to Washington to reinforce Gen. McDowell's defeated army. We were the first organized forces to reach Washington after the battle. Here, July 23rd, we were sworn into the United States service for three years. We remained around Washington until March, 1862. We were then in the second division under Gen. Geo. McCall; afterwards it was Gen. Geo. C. Meade's division. I was always under Meade. We first smelled powder Dec. 20, 1861, at the engagement at Dranesville, Va., where most of our Pa. Reserves took a hand and gained a victory at slight loss to ourselves.

We were very healthy and well this winter; we only lost one man out of a company of 101 men. As our Pa. Reserves had gone out together, we kept together and fought together the whole war.

About June, 1862, being now in the 3rd Div. of the 1st Corps, we went with McClellan's army on the Peninsular campaign in front of Richmond. The fighting commenced May 31st at Fair Oaks, but we did not get into any severe engagement until June 26th, when our division took the post of honor on the extreme right within four miles of Richmond, where from behind breastworks we repulsed the Rebel Gen. Hill and Longstreet's divisions with terrible loss to them. This was called the battle of Mechanicsville. On the morning of the 27th our corps formed a line on Gaines Hill to oppose the the three rebel divisions of Hill, Longstreet and Jackson. In this, the second of the seven days' battle before Richmond, McClellan had 20,000 to the enemy 70,000 men, and he got badly defeated, all the wounded falling into the enemy's hands. I was shot in the left arm and right side and left to the care of the enemy. Our regiment suffered the worst it ever had; we had eleven men killed out of our company alone. I was carried a prisoner of war to Richmond next day, and confined in Libby prison and also about four weeks on Belle Isle, without any surgical care more than what fellow prisoners gave me; so that after about 40 days when I was exchanged, August 6 or 7, 1862, I was able for duty and immediately joined my command in McDowell's corps at Harrison's Landing. We were soon after transferred to Gen Pope's army out on the Rappahannock, acting as a rear guard to his army from Cedar Mt, August 16th, and were the first troops to be engaged at the second battle of Bull Run, August 28, 29 and 30th. In this engagement our division was almost annihilated. The month of March before, our regiment had 1,040 officers and men, and our company a full hundred. When we retired from this fatal field the regiment could only muster 43 officers and men; my company only had myself and two others.

On September 1st occurred the battle of Chantilla, Va., where we lost two generals—Genls. Kearney and Stephens and 1,300 killed and wounded, but did not get into the engagement very much ourselves. Lieutenant Jas. Kennedy, who lives here in Lyndon, belonged to our company and had been in the rear sick with wounds, now rejoined the regiment and took charge of Co. D, and we had nine men for service. September 14th occurred the battle of South Mountain, where Lee was repulsed. We had a hand in this engagement. September 17, 1862 was fought the bloody battle of Antietam, Md. This was the end of Lee's raid on Washington. Our regiment which had 125 men, was on the extreme right and after this affair Co D consisted of five privates and no officers. But the Captain, who had been wounded, came up bringing 9 convalescents with him; and promoted me to the office of 3rd Corporal.

The next battle of importance was fought on Fredericksburg Heights, Va. Dec. 13th, under Genl. Burnside, who crossed the Rappahannock on pontoon bridges with an army of 90.000 and charged the Heights, meeting with a terrible repulse and loss of 12,000 or more men killed, wounded and missing. Here, while fighting over the second line of works, I was struck by a bullet in my left side, which disabled me for any further service for six months. Our brigade made a "forlorn hope" charge, 2,200 men going in and only 310 coming out alive and whole. Our company had 32 men, but four only were left unhurt.

I got back to my command the next summer in time to have a hand in the Gettysburg campaign. Our regiment had recruited up to 250 men, and the company had about 26 men. I was made a second sergeant. The union army laid at Fredericksburg until the rebels under Genl. Lee had marched around into the Shenandoah valley and thence across the Potomac into Pennsylvania; but we moved very rapidly when we found out their plans. Our force was 32 miles away when the first day's battle of Gettysburg came off, but we got in in time to have a hand the next morning. Our duty was to hold Little Round Top, which we did faithfully through the battle. We only lost a 2nd Lieut. here, who was shot. Lee was driven back across the Potomac and soon turned up on the Rapidann again, which was about 60 miles from Richmond towards Washington. It was a great battle ground in Virginia during the whole war.

I was in engagements with my command that fall as follows: Bristoe Station, Oct. 14th; Rappahannock Station, Nov. 7th; Mine Run. Nov. 26th, and New Hope Church. 28th. That ended our fighting until Genl. Grant started out on his Wilderness campaign. That winter of 1863 '64 we were guards on the railroad at Bristoe station.

May 5, 1864 Gen. Grant commenced his contest with Gen. Lee in the battle of the Wilderness. This was a country of dense thickets, and in three days' time the union losses were 5,000 or more killed, 21.000 or more wounded, and over 10,000 missing. We were now in the 3rd division, Gen. S. W. Crawford; 5th corps, Gen. Warren; Potomac Army, Gen. Meade. My term of service was about out, but I went into the first day's battle and was captured and carried a prisoner of war to Andersonville. I was in that horrible death hole from May 23rd to September 12, 1864, when Sherman's operations in Georgia necessitated our removal to safer quarters. We were transported then to Florence, S C. Here, in addition to starvation we had to suffer terribly from the want of any fire or protection in cold weather.

December 17, 1864 I was paroled. When I arrived at Camp Parole, Annapolis, Md., I was so gaunt and poor that I was accused by the surgeon in charge of desertion. This startled me very much until he explained that I was 'a deserter from some graveyard.' My health was ruined by the terrible prison experiences. I do not like to revert to those days, and will pass by with the remark that about all I have to show of anything that I had in the war is a wooden spoon whittled out for use there in Andersonville prison.

After I had got well enough and able to travel, I was discharged, Feb. 22, 1865, returning to my Pennsylvania home.

I came to Kansas in the spring of 1867, to Black Jack, Douglas county, making my home at Capt. Bell's. I farmed and taught school around there two years; then in company with Jim Kennedy, All Roth and others I came down to the Sac and Fox Reserve, and Feb. 28, (24) 1869 filed on our claims, which were on the mile strip 'Trust Lands.' I laid claim on the southwest ¼ section 18, townshp 17 range 16 and put up a tent there. Jim Kennedy took the next one north of me. These were all fractional quarters, containing about 130 to 137 acres each. Dave Stonebraker came down several months later and took his claim beside Kennedy's. We lived in a tent at first, on Kennedy's, and clubbed our forces together, doing some breaking; each of us had a horse, Roth. Kennedy and I. Kennedy got his house built about as it is now there on the farm, without the kitchen. He had money, and built, for those times, an unusually good house. He had married Capt. Bell's daughter and moved his family in January, 1870, and I stopped with them for nearly four years. As you remember in the war sketch, we were both in the same company in the war.

That winter or spring All Roth sold his claim out to Wm. Allison. Sr., who had come on from Canada.

I gradually improved my place and got my home ready, and March 17, 1874 I married Miss Maggie Daugherty of the neighborhood.

The children born to us from that union are all alive and all that I have —Wm. H. Weber, Estelle V. Weber, and Ollie Weber. The two oldest are graduates of our Lyndon High School, Stelle being one of the public teachers now. My wife Maggie died Dec. 24, 1884. I was a widower four years with little children, during which time my niece, Miss Anna Weber, kept the house and cared for the children most of the time. She is now Mrs. Archie Ingersoll of Lyndon.

I was elected Clerk of the District Court in the fall of 1888. I then removed to Lyndon, and Feb. 27, 1889. was married in Topeka to Miss Millie Grine, of Pennsylvania.

Owing to the change in politics in the county and state in 1890, I failed to get elected my second term, the Alliance party sweeping a good share of the offices into their care ever since.

I still live in town on my own premises, retaining my farm upon which Will Bodenhamer has lived for several years. The income from the farm, my pension and the fees of my office of Justice of the Peace, which I have held many years, more or less continuously, all make me satisfied to live and die right here in Lyndon, Kansas.

I have always been connected with the Grand Army boys here and was elected Commander of the Post in 1889. In 1891 I was elected one of the delegates from Kansas to the National Encampment at Pittsburg, which trip I enjoyed very much.

GEORGE WEBER.

Lyndon, Kansas, February, 1897.

——o——

THE OSAGE COUNTY BATTALION.

1881.

The expressed desire of the Topeka comrades, that Osage Co. send its soldiers in some kind of an organized body to attend its old soldier's reunion, Sept. 15, 1881, impelled the comrades holding office at the county seat, to hold a meeting in Aug. to see the best plan to get the soldiers together.

August 6, 1881, Warren W. Morris as President, and H. K. McConnell as Sect., J. S. Kennedy, J. H. Howe, and J. H. Sowell, as a conference committee, agreed on a plan and issued a call to the old soldiers of Osage Co.

Committees were appointed in five townships around Lyndon as follows:

Valley Brook Twp.

J. R. Hinton
F. A. Downs.
F. Ringhisen.

Junction Twp.

I. N. Morris.
Amos Cook.
Geo. McCullough.

Agency Twp.

Daniel Hare.
Joe Marshall.
Robert Neil.

Melvern Twp.

Maj. Jumper.
Capt. Opdycke.
O. S Starr.

Fairfax Twp.

B. G. Wilson.
James Newton.
Amos Worrell.

These committees were requested to work up enthusiasm among the old soldiers and turn out September 3rd at Lyndon for a mass meeting, and try and effect an organization among them as a regim nt.

Lyndon immediately set to work to organize a company of veterans. The Grand Army Post did not seem to be in harmony that year with the old boys, so Capt. Whirey went ahead and organized this company of 60 or more old veterans, as will be seen on page 113.

After the comrades at the county seat had issued their notices and called a mass meeting at Lyndon September 3, 1881. The Osage City comrades insisted on a change and we got their hearty support. The place of meeting was changed to Osage City for the date agreed upon above. Capt. Admire, T. L. Marshall and others threw their influence in and secured the attendance there, Sept. 3rd, of Maj. Tom Anderson and Captain Joe Waters. It was a rousing big meeting of old soldiers from all round the county. Lew Finch of Burlingame, was chairman; J. V. Admire, Secretary and committee on publication. After the speaking was through a committee reported the following names as suitable persons to officer the proposed

OSAGE COUNTY BATTALION:

H. K. McConnell..........Colonel,
Harrison Dubois........Lieut. Col,
Geo. W. Morris.............Major,
Chas. Cochran...............Adjt,
W. C. Sweezey...............Surg.
Chas. Foulks.................Q. M.

I find the Lyndon Leader of September 8th full of military notices.

Superintendent McConnell, as Col., issues notices to the old boys about the time of starting up to the Topeka Reunion and about the Battalion falling in at the Topeka depot for march to the Reunion grounds. A special early morning train from Emporia September 15th landing the boys there at 8:30 A. M.

The Lyndon Cornet Band in good organization and one of the best out of a half dozen leading bands of the State, headed our Lyndon Veteran Company, which at Topeka all merged into the one Battalion. Not being present that year of 1881, I cannot sp ak further but the old boys came home fairly enthused with the good times touching elbows with each other once more.

That December Andy Cotterman was elected Commander of the Post to serve in 1882. Capt. Whinrey's veteran company disbanded and thereafter the several Grand Army Posts in Osage County went to make up the Osage County Battalion.

The next mass meeting of old soldiers was held in Lyndon August 31, 1882. A preliminary meeting was held Aug. 11th at Osage City, at which Sim Bradford presided. There were five Grand Army Post in the county then and they resolved to have Senator Plumb invited to speak to the old soldiers at Lyndon the 31st, if agreeable all round.

Col. A. K. McConnell called the Osage County Battalion together with all old soldiers to meet at Lyndon on that date.

The Lyndon Leader contains such a good account of the program and doings that I copy it all into my book:

PROGRAM.

All Posts of G. A. R. and all old soldiers will meet at the hall of Lyndon Post at 10:30 o'clock A. M., where the procession will immediately form and march through the principal streets to the M. E. church under the direction of the officers of the day, headed by the Cornet and Military Bands.

ORDER OF EXERCISES.

Prayer.
Song by the Choir,
Address 'Welcome,'. P. C. Lyndon Post.
Response........P. C. Carbondale Post.
Song, 'Army Beans'..........by Choir.
Invocation......Rev. G. W. Browning.
Bugle call.

DINNER.

Bugle call, 'Fall in.'
Address................by Col. Plumb,
Music by Band.
'Our National Flag'..Rev. Oscar Green.
'Boys in Blue'.............J. M. Asher,
Song, 'Brave Boys are They'.
'Sanitary Commission' Dr. C. W. Sweezey
'Our Fallen Comrades' Dr. L. W. Schenk
Song by the Choir,
'Grand Army of the Republic,'........
............Genl. H. K. McConnell,
'The Camp'......Dr. W. J. Washburn,
Song, 'Tenting on the Old Camp Ground'
'The Field'..........Hon. C. S. Martin,
'The March'.........Maj A. H. Jumper
Song 'Marching Through Georgia,'
'Army of the Frontier and Southwest'..
.....................W. W. Morris,
'Government Mule'.......E. G. Russel,
Song, 'Old Shady,'
'Southern Loyalists'.........J. R. Poe,
'Prisoners of War'..........L. E. Finch,
Song, 'Tramp, Tramp, Tramp,'
'Coming Home'..........J. V. Admire,
Martial Music, 'Johny Comes Marching Home'

Come everybody and will have a good time. Other prominent speakers will be present, from home and abroad.

J. T. UNDERWOOD,
J. H. HOWE, Com.
W. W. MORRIS,

Following is the report of the proceedings as copied from the Leader of August 31, 1882:

GALA DAY.

A Large Crowd and a Good Time.

"It is the biggest day Lyndon ever saw, is what everyone said. It is a day that will be remembered by both young and old.

The morning opened cold with a light rain and it looked for awhile that the weather would prevent the attendance of any great number from a distance, but as the day anvanced the clouds lightened and the people began to arrive, so that by half past ten the visiting posts had arrived.

"By eleven o'clock the line of procession had been formed by the marshals and they moved. The column being made up as follows:

Marshal J. R. Drew, Assistant Marshal J. T. Underwood, Lyndon Cornet Band, Jim Bain leader; Lyndon Post No. 19, with 65 men commanded by J. M. Whitney; Osage City Martial Band, Osage City Post No. 11, with 50 men commanded by T. L Marshal, carriage containing Senator Plumb, Postmaster Whittemore and Treasurer John Rankin, carriage with Mayor Keenan and J. H. Savely, Burlingame Cornet Band W. C. Chatfield, leader, Burlingame Post No. 35, with 35 men commanded by J. H. Burke, Carbondale Post No. 94, with 25 men, commanded by S. B. Bradford.

"The procession paraded some of our streets, which were thronged with people from every part of the county.

"The column finally halted at the new Methodist church where the exercises of the day were to be held. The audience room was already filled with the exception of the seats reserved for the soldiers. W. A. Cotterman, commander of the Lyndon Post, G. A. R., was master of the ceremonies, and after the meeting was opened with prayer by Rev. W. W. Curtis, he delivered an address of welcome, which was responded to by S. B. Bradford, of Carbondale.

After the choir, consisting of Mrs. Bowman, the Misses Whitman, Tweed and Blake and Messrs. Towers, Henderson and Drew with Mrs. Etta Howe as organist, had rendered some music, the bugle sounded "Dinner," which was served in the basement of the church to a large and hungry multitude and yet there was plenty left.

"In the afternoon the main address was made by Senator Plumb, who spoke for an hour and a quarter, delivering an interesting speech on the soldier's life, which was replete with anecdote and full of pathos. The Senator was listened to by at least one thousand persons, who frequently applauded his remarks and cheered him heartily when he had finished.

The only toasts that were responded to were those of Dr. Sweezey, on the 'Sanitary Commission' and Dr. Schenck, on 'Our Fallen Comrades.' Time would not permit the hearing of others.

A meeting of the old soldiers was then held and a committee was appointed to select officers for the county battalion the ensuing year. The committee reported in favor of

Major J. H. Burke, Burlingame Post, for Colonel; S. B. Bradford, Carbondale Post, Lieut. Col; D. H. Danhauer, Lyndon Post, Major; T. L. Marshal, Osage City Post, Quarter Master. These gentlemen were elected.

Colonel McConnell then in a neat speech turned the command over to the new commander, who at once took charge of the battalion.

It was decided to go to Topeka on the 13th of September The battalion then marched to the headquarters of the Lyndon Post, where they broke ranks after giving three cheers for the Lyndon Post, the people of Lyndon and Col. McConnell."

The history of the battalion in succeeding years—1883-'84 is but a repetition of 1881-'82. Many of our prominent county soldiers have held office in the battalion; and at the Topeka Reunions, at Leavenworth in 1884, and on other occasions it made the old soldiers of the county feel proud when, with our two or three brass bands from Lyndon, Osage City and Burlingame, and all the Grand Army Posts with their banners and men we strung out 400 in number.

The five Posts alluded to in 1882 were

Post No. 11, Osage City,
Post No. 19, Lyndon.
Post No. 35, Burlingame,
Post No. 67, Scranton,
Post No. 94, Carbondale.

In 1893 I find three more Posts noticed, that had been organized several years then, viz:

Post No. 221, Quenemo,
Post No. 237, Overbrook.
Post No. 238, Melvern.

All these Posts are active and doing good work now, as far as I know.

——o——

The day for the necessity of an organization like the Osage County Battalion is past, for it has been at least eight years that I know of since any gathering.

SKETCHES OF THE LIVES OF A. M. SANDERSON AND C. R. GREEN, TENTH AND ELEVENTH COMMANDERS OF LYNDON POST.

——o——

A. M. SANDERSON.

At the request of the historian, Comrade Sanderson, who was the tenth Commander of Lyndon Post No. 19 Kansas, contributed the following

SKETCH:

I was born near Massillon, Stark county, Ohio, June 24, 1835, and cast my first vote for John C. Fremont for President—(1856).

I left Ohio during the fall of 1854, going to Leesburg, Kosciusko county, Indiana. November 14, 1856 I was married to Elizabeth Edman, my present wife I enlisted in Co E, 12 Ind. Infantry, under Capt. Reuben Williams (now Brig. General), Oct. 9, 1861.

I had plenty of work, and was making from $3.00 to $5.00 a day, but believing every one who possibly could should go and help defend our flag and constitution of the best government the sun ever shone on, I gave up my work and enlisted.

Having made up my mind to enlist, I went home and told my wife. She said while she dreaded to have me go, if I felt it to be my duty, she would not say nay; and with a "God bless and care for you," I was off for the war, leaving her and the child to get along alone. I went to Indianapolis, thence we went direct to "Dam No. 4" on the Potomac river, Md., where we helped guard that stream, mainly to keep articles contraband of war from being crossed over to Virginia. At that time salt was worth only $10.00 per bushel; quinine the same per ounce.

During January, 1862 there was an

attempt made to destroy Dam No. 4 as it was a feeder to the canal by which much forage and supp ies were shipped to Harper's Ferry. During this exchange of shot and shell our Capt., with 10 boys while reconoiteri g got surrounded by rebel cava'ry and were taken prisoners. This was on the upper Potomac, above Harpers Ferry.

In February, 1862 we crossed the Potomac at Williamsport, Md., and moved to M rtinsburg, Va, thence to Bunker Hill, where we met some rebel cavalry hard. From there we moved slowly, sometimes camping as high as three times in the same place. From Bunker Hill to Winchester it was one continuous skirmish. The night before we entered Winchester we camped in an open field without our tents, but well supplied with amunition, (as though an extra 20 rounds could warm us). We were completely worn out and glad of the chance of resting our weary bodies. In the morning on waking we found we had an extra b'anket of about 4 inches of snow. After hot coffee and hard tack we were ordered to pile knapsacks and overcoats, form a line and go for the breastworks north of town. Dur ng the night the enemy had evacuated and we only captured about 20 stragglers. From here we started east, Gen Shields in command, the morning of the fight which occurred in the afternoon at Winchester, we crossed the Shenandoah, at Snick r's Ferry by fording. It was from 3 to 4 feet deep, rocky bottom, very uneven and by no means hot. Near Aldee, a small town on the east side of the mountain, we stopped long enough to bury a comrade who was in some way poisoned; supposedly by eating some provisions bought from citizens.

Our next point was M nasses, thence to Culpepper; then to a small town where Johnson had winter d h's army. It was here I saw my first Quaker guns mounted on the breastworks. Our next and final stop was at Warrenton Junction, where we relieved Blenker and his men, who, by the way, had been subsisting off the country They had eaten everything but fence rails, and had commenced on them. Here we remained until May; our time having expired, we were shipped to Wash ngton in box cars, where we were in due time discharged and returned home.

When I think of sleeping under snow at Winchester, waking up in the night on Bull Run battlefield, the water running through our tent four inches deep; lying on our guns at Dam No. 4 in an old log barn, the wind howling a perfect hurricane, not daring to speak above a whisper, expecting to be fired on every moment; then out on picket at Williamsport, the murcury 12 below zero, no fire and all you could do to keep the wind from stealing your blanket; again on picket on the Potomac, where it is 270 yards wide, it makes me shudder to go over the old times again when it was cold enough to form an ice from shore to shore during one day and night, and where we had to relieve one-another every 10 or 15 minutes to keep from freezing to death; these and many other exposures I could relate, I do not wonder that we have to end our days in suffering. No, my citizen friend and neighbor, you never did, nor you never can realize what we passed through and what we now are suffering. May the time never come when our children or their children shall be called on to go in defense of our country. But should it come, do not fear or shirk your duty. Honor and support our glorious banner—the stars and stripes under any and all circumstances.

A. M. SANDERSON.

Mr. Sanderson's occupation in life has been one of handling tools as well as farming, being a carpenter and wagon maker.

He left Indiana the fall of 1884, living the first winter in Shawnee county. Next spring he moved onto a piece of land he bought in Arvonia township on the Marais des Cygnes river, being the west 80 of northeast quarter, section 17, township 18, range 17. living there four years. He then came to his present home in Lyndon, and has followed his occupation of carpentry and wagon repairing ever since.

Mr. Sandersons have had eleven children born to them, of which five died in early childhood. There are three boys and three girls alive, all but the oldest living in or near Lyndon. Four are married and in homes of their own, as follows:

Ann Launa Sanderson, the oldest alive, was married May 6, 1886 to Dr. J. G. L. Myers, and lives at Bloomingdale, Ind. They have six children.

Sarah Miriam Sanderson was married April 25, 1889 to Fred N. Davis of Lebo, Kansas. They have one child and live here in Lyndon.

Milton Edman Sanderson married July 21, 1890 to Miss Madge Hazlerig of Burlington, Kansas. They live in Lyndon and have a family of four children.

Austin Leon Sanderson was married July 13, 1896 to Miss Katie A. Rice, daughter of Cam Rice, 4 miles east of Lyndon, near where they have settled.

Emilie Marie Sanderson was one of the seven of the first graduating class in 1895 of the Lyndon High School and at the present time is successfully conducting the Panteg school in this county. Her home is with her parents in Lyndon.

Harold Markley Sanderson is a youth of 16, at home and attending the High School.

C. R. GREEN.

The Eleventh Commander of Lyndon Post—1895.

Charles R. Green was born November 8, 1845 at Milan, Erie county, Ohio. He was raised in Wakeman and Clarksfield townships, Huron county, Ohio, where his father followed farming and the son, the eldest in a family of ten, got what common school education one could under such circumstances.

Being alive to the issues that brought on the war, he tried to go in the fall of 1861 as a soldier in the 55th Ohio, which was recruiting around him, but his father objected as he was only a lad, less than 16 years old.

The next summer, when, after the 7 days' battles by McClellan's army in front of Richmond, in July, President Lincoln issued his call for 200,000 more volunteers, Comrade Green, though only then a lad of 16½ years and 133 pounds weight, enlisted August 8, 1862, in Co. A, 101st Ohio Volunteers, for 3 years or during the war. The father did not consent, however, to his son's going until after he had been examined by a county medical board and got his exemption papers, as, being under 45 years of age, he was otherwise subject to draft. So after taking this precaution for the welfare of the family, the father was willing to let Charles go to the war. Nine enlisted in the 101st Ohio from Charles Green's home-town, Clarksfield, that August.

The following summary of their service is only one of ten thousand such cases from towns all over the land, in the war of the Rebellion,

Watson Rowland died January 31, 1863 at Nashville.

Henry Fish died at Murfreesboro, Tenn, April 25, 1863.

Clark Barber died July 7, 1863 at Louisville, Ky.

Charles Scott, killed May 19, '64, Atlanta campaign.

Byron Scott was never mustered.

Edwin W. Cunningham was discharged from field service by reason of disability in 1863, but at the same time was commissioned a United States hospital steward in the regular army, which office he filled a year or more, when be resigned and returned home to his studies, and came to Emporia, Kansas in an early day, where he is known as Judge Cunningham at the present writing.

Levi O. Rowland received bad wounds at the battle of Stone River, December 31, 1862. He remained about 14 months in the hospital, when February 15, 1864 he was discharged, and has been a sufferer from the same disability ever since.

Myron Furlong was discharged February 10, 1863 on surgeons certificate of disability.

This disposes of eight, and the Ohio Book of Records, Vol. 7 goes on to state that Charles R. Green was mustered out with his company at the end of the war, June 12, 1865, the only one of the nine who was able to see the war through and come home with his command; not by reason of strength and health, but by an overruling Providence which singles out some to death and others to lifelong suffering—some to glory and others to sorrow.

The 101st Ohio's first service in Dixie was to help repel Gen. Kirby Smith's rebel raid on Covington, Kentucky and Cincinnati, Ohio. Here is where Gov. Todd of Ohio, in September, '62 called on the men of his state to rally at once in the defense of their homes. The forces who volunteered on that occasion were called "squirrel hunters." When the danger was over at this point the many regiments of new soldiers called to Covington from Ohio and Indiana were transferred to Louisville and October 1st to 3rd, put into the old brigades of Genl. Buell's army and soon marched out to the battle of Perryville, Ky., Oct. 7th and 8th.

The 101st did not shed any blood here, although under fire. They were put into Gen. Carlin's brigade of Genl. Jeff C. Davis' division, Gen. A. D. McCook's corps, Rosecran's army. They remained in this organization until after the battle of Chickamauga, and through the whole war had as fellow comrades in the brigade, Grant's old regiment, the 21st Ill., the 38th Ill., and the 81st Ind.

When the 101st Ohio Infantry was put into this brigade of soldiers at Louisville, the old regiments had seen almost a year's active service and had fought many battles and skirmishes and to have a regiment a thousand strong put with them was a God-send indeed. Scorning to carry a knapsack or blanket in the summer; desiring but the one shirt to their backs, they came in from their long chase after Bragg, up from Iuka, Miss., ragged, dirty, locks unshorn, lousy with graybacks, adebt in the art of living off the country. Their officers even boasting that their men could stop, slaughter a hog or cook a cup of coffee and not interrupt the day's steady march. Such were the companions who kindly looked the new levies over and shouted "fresh fish" on that Ky. march of '62, and who considerately allowed them to carry blankets and knapsacks in the day time, that the old soldiers might have their contents to use the next night. The new troops soon found this game out, and also the folly of carrying such heavy loads. The 81st Ind., which took their place in the brigade that fall in the place of Col. Heg's Norwegian regiment, the 15th Wisconsin, transferred, was also a new regiment, and both had to put up with the old soldiers' abuse and ridicule several months, until the battle of Stone River baptized them in blood, the 101st proving their heroism by leaving half their number on the battlefield.

The Kentucky march had been a long, wearisome one to the new soldiers —from Louisville to Nashville, made in dry weather with a good many deviations or side trips, and the sudden change of weather, which, October 26th brought snow to the depth of several inches. This occurred while they were encamped at Rolling Forks and caused much sickness from the exposure, and before they got down into Tennessee ready for the battle of Stone River the 101st Ohio was reduced to less than one-half effective men for duty, and company A, to which Mr. Green belonged, which had left Ohio with 96 men, and in November had 44 men, entered their first real battle with only 28 men for duty.

At the beginning of the battle, December 26th, all men not able to stand the march and exposure were ordered to the rear with the wagon train, so that Mr. Green, being among this number, missed the heaviest days' battle—December 31st, but hearing of the almost total annihilation of his regiment, joined the army at the front in time to be in the last two days' battle, and when he found his company nine men only were left, and only 110 in the regiment. Both Colonels and other officers of the companies were killed or wounded. Nearly all the wounded and many others were taken prisoners. In a day or two enough stragglers came up to make over 200 present. The fighting before and after lasted six days and at its close the battle field with all the union dead and many of the rebels fell to the union army. Here Comrade Green helped to bury one of their own mess and 12 others of the regiment, all in one wide grave, on the battle field.

The union army camped around Murfreesboro the next six months. The people thought Genl. Rosecrans with his magnificent union army of 50,000 men would never get started southward again, but the 24th of June, '63 found the army in motion, and active campaigning was going on until after the battle of Chickamauga. Mr. Green was all through the campaign with his regiment, and in the battle of Chickamauga got hit in three places two of the wounds being through each arm. From a regiment numbering 225 before, the end of the battle left them 65 men present for duty, and Co. A was reduced from 17 to 3 men, several being killed or badly wounded and left on the battlefield. Comrade Green's wounds were such as did not hinder his getting away, and he was absent six months back in Nashville and Ohio recovering from his wounds, getting two furloughs home in the meantime. In February, 1863, his arms not being strong enough to carry a gun, the medical authorities at Cincinnati thought to transfer him into the Invalid Veteran Reserve Corps, an organization in the rear to do guard duty over prisoners, recruits, commissary stores, etc. But Mr. Green concluded that if they wanted his services to help put down the war, it must be at the front; so he took such a course that he fell into disgrace with the doctors, and as a punishment they ordered him sent to the front to rejoin his command at Chattanooga, the very thing, that he privately was working for; and, although not able for duty, he became so by the time Old Billy Sherman started the army out for the 100-days fighting of the Atlanta campaign.

As usual, the very first battle they got into, which was a charge on Buzzards' Roost, their company lost several men, the Lieut commanding company and Orderly Sergeant both being killed, and all through the rest of that campaign the company never had over ten men, and for three weeks in front of Kenesaw Mountain, three men only for duty, C. R. Green being one of them. There were four more present, but two were detailed in the Pioneer Corps and two were non-commissioned officers. The company was attached to another company because there were no spare officers for it; and, to cut a long story short, it never had more than 14 or 16 men present again to the end of the war.

When the Atlanta campaign was over the Army of the Cumberland under Genl. Thomas, was detached to march back into Tennessee and defend it against Hood's raid, while "Sherman marched down to the sea."

The 101st Ohio was in Col. Kirby's Brigade, Genl. Stanley's Division, Gen O. O. Howard's 4th Army Corps in the most of the Atlanta campaign. When McPherson was killed, July 22, 1864, Howard was placed in command of the Army of the Tennessee, and Genl Stanley took the 4th Corps. But at the battle of Nashville and to the end of the war Genl. Thomas J. Wood commanded the 4th Corps, and when Genl. David S. Stanley was promoted, Gen. Nathan Kimball took the Division and was its commander until the end of the war. Col. I. N. Kirby was the 101st Ohio's Colonel from the battle of Stone River to the end of the war, nearly, but on part of the Atlanta campaign—the Franklin and Nashville days and to the end, he commanded the brigade, and was made a general at the last, richly meriting the promotion.

Comrade Green was hit three times by missiles of war in the Georgia campaign but not serious enough to cause his falling out. Along in the fall of '64 the constant exposure and fatigue of a wet November while they were marching back into Tennessee, guarding and assisting along a wagon train of a thousand wagons more or less, over the Cumberland Mountains, so bore down on his heretofore rugged constitution that he came down sick with that dreadful army disease known as the "chronic diarrhœa," and was ordered to the Nashville hospital only the day before the battle of Franklin where his regiment suffered a loss of a few men only, and in the battle of Nashville, December 15 and 16, '64, where Genl. Thomas so signally defeated Hood's rebel army, the regiment lost 10 men.

Mr. Green was away three months recovering his health Having been transferred to Ohio hospitals, he had a furlough home, which was undoubtedly the saving of his life.

The custom was by the army doctors then to give plenty of opium and quinine and other equally strong drugs. Mr. Green, seeing that he did not recover by the hospital treatment, soon took the practice of eating roasted cheese and crackers and drinking scalded milk, regularly turning into the spit box the doses left by the doctors.

In March, 1865 he rejoined his regiment at Huntsville, Ala., and the whole corps was soon transferred to East Tennessee, where they had to guard against a possibility of Genl. Lee's escape from Richmond via Lynchburg into Tennessee. Here the end of the war found them, and soon after they were transferred to Nashville, and June 12th mustered out. They went in a body to Cleveland, Ohio, where, on June 20. 1865. they received their pay and were discharged.

Mr. Green served 3 years, lacking 40 days as a private. He now returned home to Clarksfield, Ohio.

AFTER THE WAR.

The war was over and here was C. R. Green, less than 20 years old, with three years' experience in battling for himself alone and with 500 dollars of his war money, but a great 3-year gap in his education stared him in the face, which he at once set out to fill by two years' attendance at the Milan, Ohio Normal School and a term of teaching school. not quitting until he was able to pass second grade in their coun'y examinations.

April, 1867, in his 22d year, he followed Horace Greeley's advice to young men by coming out to Kansas "to grow up with the country." He landed in the Kaw river bottoms at Lenape, Leavenworth county, Kansas, where an uncle, James P. Green, was operating three steam saw mil's to furn sh timber for a hundred miles of the Union Pacific Railway from Junction City westward. The Delaware and Wyandotte Indians had just disposed of their reserves but had not moved to the Territory, and "the noble red man" was about the first attraction seen by Mr. Green in Kansas on stepping off the cars.

After spending about two months with his uncle, who in the meantime removed to the "State Line" bottom of Kansas City. Missouri, which in '67 had the State Line depot and very few other buildings on it, the last of May, '67 he concluded to go across the plains to California.

Mr. Green got a position with a surveying party and went out across the plains, through New Mexico, Arizona and California to the Pacific coast. It was a preliminary railway survey and exploring expedition run by the Union Pacific R. W. E. D. and the Government. The latter sending out a scientific party who discovered and reported the great coal fields of Trinidad and the Raton Mountains, and who paved the way for Major Powell's geological survey of the Great Canon of the Colorado a few years later.

The Santa Fe railroad some of the way runs over the route that Mr. Green helped to survey in 1867-'68, for he was about a year absent from Kansas, returning by Old Mexico. Panama and New York.

This was a very interesting trip in the days of the Santa Fe Trail, the Overland Stage, Indian war and "Custer on the Plains." They were at Old Kit Carson's abode in the Rocky Mountains, and the many adventures and tales about this trip Mr. Green will put in a chapter to itself.

When he came back to Kansas in 1868 he spent three months with his uncle at Kansas City, h lpi g to make some of the first buildings of the boom on those great bottoms, before there was any Union Depot there. In August, getting tired of city life, he went up on the Delaware Reserve in Leavenworth county, half way between Lawrence and Leavenworth and bought himself a farm and went to teaching in the country schools. He taught more or less steadily the next six years, improving his farm and living on it, so that one day when a man offered him $3,800 for it he replied. "No, you can have it for $4,000. and not a cent less," but he would give possession at once of all crops, and the house. May 17, '73 the sale was made and in a few months Mr. Green closed up his business and term of school and took his family, consisting of wife and two children, and April, 1874 removed to Clarksfield, Ohio, three thousand dollars the richer for his Kansas experience. They were renters two years on their Father Green's farm, when they bought a farm of their own in Wakeman, and lived there four years.

But six years in Ohio made him and his wife homesick for the western people and opportunities to get ahead and they came back again, this time buying and settling down on a farm in the Dane neighborhood, six miles west of Quenemo and four and a half south east of Lyndon, Osage county.

Mr. Green did not wish to settle down again in Leavenworth county. The taxes were very high there and the price of land four times as much as in newer counties. He carefully looked over ten counties in 1879 before locating, and never regretted his final choice of Osage county. He lost considerable by the move to Ohio, but gained experience. He settled here June 20, 1880.

He married December 28, 1869 in Tama county, Iowa Flavia Barbour, a playmate of his in Ohio before the war. Six children, three girls and three boys, were born to them from this union, when death claimed the wife, March 21, 1883, at the age of 35, leaving a little babe which Mr. Green gave to a sister in Ohio.

The oldest of these children, Mary Alice Green, was married to Albert I. Haskins, of Wakeman, Ohio, in 1893 and lives there. The eldest son, Ovid Elias Green, died September 15, 1889 at the age of 13. A little girl, Jennie Alda, died in 1885 aged 4. So that, not counting the two children in Ohio, Mr. Green has only two at home, Winifred B. Green, a young lady graduate of the "Class '95," Lyndon High School and a teacher of the county, and Norman B. Green, a young man of 19.

For his second wife Mr. Green married November 17, 1887 Miss Annie Kring, one of his old Leavenworth county school pupils.

Mr. Green resides in a comforable home a mile or two south of Lyndon. Being interested in horticulture, he has large orchards and acres of forest trees, vines, etc. He has built himself plenty of barns and other outbuildings, and a good house with a large fire-proof library and museum room, so that he has no desire whatever to leave the farm for town life.

Always taking naturally to tools he has saved hundreds of dollars doing all of his own building; and he finds that good buildings and sheltered tools and stock are good investments on a farm, and that though a man may love other pursuits in life and follow them for a season, there is nothing compared to the peace and happiness and independence of living on a pleasantly located farm. And while he tried Florida one winter season for his health, he found on his return here that Kansas, wayward as she is in many things, best suits him out of the 27 states and territories that he has been in during the last 40 years. And being the best to live in, all things considered, certainly then it is good enough to die in.

PRISON LIFE IN DIXIE.

WM. HAAS' WAR STORY.

Wm. Haas was born November 17, 1836 in Shenandoah county, Va. He left Virginia with his parents in 1838 or '39 for Harrison county, Ind., and went for himself altogether about 1858, settling in Knox, the northeast county of Missouri.

In his language he says:

"I enlisted in the 1st Battalion Mo. Home Guards, which afterwards went to make up the 21st Mo. Inft. about May 1, 1861. We were only about 300 in number in the state service for 6 months, and had our hands full saving North Missouri to the Union. We were guarding railroad trains, bridges, and preventing rebel recruiting officers from running off men to the rebel army. We were never south of the Missouri river. Towards the last of my service I was sick and did not enlist with these battalions of the State service into the U. S., constituting the 21st Mo. Inft. My family was then at Laomi, near Springfield, Ill., so when discharged about Nov. 1, '61 at Canton, Lewis county, Mo., I joined my family in Illinois.

I enlisted in the U. S. service at Springfield, Ill., in Co. B. 130th Inft the 20th of Aug., 1862. Col. Niles commanding. We were mustered and drilled at Camp Butler, remaining there until November 1, 1862. We were then transferred to Memphis and put on provost duty part of the time during the winter of '62 3. We belonged to McClernand's command, 13th Army Corps, A. J. Smith's Div, and went down to Milliken's Bend with Grant's Vicksburg expedition the early part of the spring, where with thousands of other new troops we lost a great many from sickness and exposure in that swamp country opposite Vicksburg.

About April, 1863 we broke camp and crossed over the 30 or 40-mile neck of land made by the Mississippi river there and came out below Vicksburg, still on the west bank. But enough transports and steamers had run the gauntlet of rebel batteries and got down to our assistance so that Genl. Grant was able to immediately cross his army to the eastern shore below Vicksburg and give battle to the rebel forces, first at Magnolia Hill, where we only got in at the tail end as a support to a battery. Champion Hills and Black River engagements followed in quick succession, enabling the union army to divide the rebel forces into two armies and forcing Gen. Pemberton's command back into Vicksburg. At Black River, May 17th, we made a charge through a swamp and caused the rebels to surrender.

"I got hit by a bullet the 19th of May but the wound was not serious enough to separate me from my command.

About the 22nd of May Genl Oard superceded Genl. McClernand in the command of the 13th Army Corps. On this day there was a general charge of the union forces on the rebel works of Vicksburg, but we could not take them, and there was a terrible loss of killed and wounded that day. We lost 14 killed out of our regiment. We were now in very close quarters at the siege of Vicksburg. The rifle pits where the skirmishers or pickets watched against any sudden dash of the enemy were but a few yards in advance of the main breastworks, and we went and came from these pits only in the night time as it was instant death to expose our persons in daylight. The siege lasted until July 4, 1863, when Genl. Pemberton surrendered Vicksburg and his whole army, which Genl. Grant paroled to their southern homes, but many of them disregarded their paroles and were found fighting again for the Southern cause at Chickamauga, September, '63, before they had been exchanged.

"After the Vicksburg campaign, being sick with chronic diarrhœa and dropsy, I got a furlough home. I was so bad that I had to be hauled from the cars home, but after two or three months I got well and joined my regiment which was now about 100 miles west of New Orleans in the sugar country at New Iberia, La. Some time in December, 1863 we went back to Algiers near New Orleans and embarked on a steamer and steamed down into the Gulf of Mexico and around into Metagorda Bay, coast of Texas, where we laid in camp all winter. March, '64 we embarked again and went to Berwick Bay on the same coast, but nearer to Genl. Banks' objective point in the Red River campaign of that year. There were of our 13th Corps, which was now commanded by Genl. Ransom, two divisions. Our division was commanded by Genl. Vance.

"There was a rebel army in Texas and Western La. commanded by Genls. Kirby Smith and Dick Taylor, the whole object of the Red River campaign, which had been gradually working up for months, was to whip the rebel forces here and end the war west of the Mississippi river.

"We marched up the country, our division in advance and Genl. Ransom commanding. At Sabine X Roads near Mansfield in De Soto county, La., a good many days' march from the coast, we were attacked by the rebel forces and cut off from the rest of the army under Banks, which had not left camp that day, and there occurred the battle of Sabine X Roads.

"Our forces numbered 2,300 at the front while the rebels had 8,600. Genl. Ransom was badly wounded at the start and Genl. Vance taking command was killed, so that we labored under much confusion, and when towards night the rebels surrounded us, although we had been fighting all day, and Banks did not reinforce us, we had no other alternative than to surrender. Lots of the union troops got through the rebel lines, so that they only captured 1144 prisoners. But it took about all our regiment as well as others in our brigade. There was quite a loss of killed and wounded. This engagement was April 8, 1864. We surrendered about sundown and were hurried off across the country to Camp Ford near Tyler, Texas. Banks with all his forces retreated and thus ingloriously ended the great Red River campaign.

"We were in prison 414 days, until May 27, 1865, the end of the war. Jas. Henton, who had enlisted in the same company and regiment with me at Springfield, Ill., was a fellow prisoner at Camp Ford. We had ten acres of a sandy knoll for a camp, fenced with split logs eleven feet long, set on end in a trench so that eight feet stuck up above the surface of the ground on the inside of the stockade, while on the outside the rebels had earth banked up half way, so that there was a good path for the guards to walk along on and their heads be two feet above the wall. Thus with their guns ever on guard a few men could watch four or five thousand of us. While there was plenty of timber in the country around, they would not allow us to get any of it for shelter from the sun's rays--fuel we could get. When the weather got cold in November they allowed us to go out under guard to cut and bring in timber from which we rove out shakes and made ourselves little shelters. In the battle we had taken off our knapsacks that contained our blankets and oil-cloths, and when captured no one had any such article scarcely in our regiment. As we were being hurried off to the prison I saw a man of the 77th Ill with a woolen blanket tied around him and I offered him $5 for it, which he refused; then I increased my bid, finally giving him a ten dollar greenback for it. This was all the blanket that was in our whole company there in prison that season. As the heat of summer came on we fastened it up with some little poles so that several of us could crawl under it out of the dews and heat. No one can ever comprehend the endless misery of thousands of us, held there in that 10-acre prison-house of death that 14 months. The only relieving qualities being good air and sunshine and plenty of nice spring water running out into three long troughs, sufficient for all purposes. When we first went there, there were only two or three hundred prisoners in it, but the captures from our division, from A. J. Smith's command of the 16th corps and of a force of Gen. Steele's army up in Arkansas, all operating under Banks in the Red River campaign, soon swelled our number several thousands and the stockade had to be enlarged at once. The largest number at one time being 4,500 prisoners; healthy when captured; but confine a large number of men to a meager diet and see how quick disease works havoc. Scurvy and chronic diarrhœa soon lead all other sicknesses. We were fed mostly on corn meal and some beef. Fuel and salt were both very scarce.

They could never count us very correctly. They would vary from 300 to 500 of getting a correct count. On account of rations it being to our interest to appear more numerous. A quarter of beef weighing 80 pounds had to supply rations to one ward of 300 men. There were so many squads, so that after the bones had all been broken up and the beef cut into small pieces 10 or 15 piles would be made of that quarter and each one as near equal to the other as possible, and while one turned his back another one would place his hand on the pile and ask the one with his back turned whose that should be and whatever mess was named had to accept that as a fair division of the days' issue. Our regimental Quartermaster acted inside for all the forces.

The rebel commander of the camp, Col. Jennison, once while away left the camp in charge of his Adjutant, McCann. The boys would play Keno inside, and he would come in and steal their pile of money on the gambling board and then order them to disperse. The boys afterwards when they saw him coming would shout 'Keno' to each other so as to be on their guard. One morning as he was riding by camp on the outside some one hollowed 'Keno!' and then for fun the whole camp took it up. That night McCann, to punish them, withheld their rations, and all the next day they got none. Towards night our Q. M., Johnson, went out to ask the reason why we got no rations and McCann replied that he intended to to starve the d—d Yanks out for hollowing Keno. Johnson vouched to him for the whole camp that they should no more hollow 'Keno.' The boys agreed to it, so the next morning they got their rations.

"Sometime about May 12, 1865 the whole force of prisoners were marched and hauled 120 miles to Shreveport, La., on the Red river, where we took steamer down that stream to the Mississippi. Here the rebels turned us over to the U. S., at a camp on the east bank where, as we landed under the old Union flag, we marched by a row of cracker boxes and got our fill once more. Thence to New Orleans where we were able to clean up and draw new clothing, mostly by aid of the Sanitary Commission. We stayed here a week, then were transferred up the Mississippi to Jefferson Barracks at St. Louis. Here we drew our commutation money, i e, 25 cents a day for rations not furnished us by Uncle Sam while in prison. I received $103.50. From there we Illinois soldiers went to Springfield, Ill., where we were mustered out and paid off June 24, 1865. And this was the end of my war service, but it left me sick, scurvy in my limbs, chronic diarrhœa in my system, as well as an awful cough, which ailments I have never entirely got over yet."

WM. HAAS.

LYNDON GUARDS.

J. H. STAVELY, CAPT.

1881.

The organization of the Valley Brook Veteran Company at Lyndon about September 5, 1881 by Capt. Whinrey and others as one of the companies of the Osage County Battalion so inaugurated a martial spirit here in Lyndon that the boys, young men and men of middle age caught the desire to be organized into a company for drill and use upon occasions of public necessity. In fact the young men organized into a militia company similar to the one at that time in Burlingame.

This company was called the "Lyndon Guards." I do not know who was instrumental in getting it up, but I presume from the fact that Joseph H. Stavely, George W. Morris, of the firm Fairbanks & Morris, and James W. Bain, the leader of the Cornet Band, were elected officers, that they were at the inception of the movement as was R. A. Miller and Harry Rogers. Upon talking with Mr. Stavely about it recently, he said that all memoranda of its organization and list of members seemed to be lost; that it numbered 60 members; that the company failed to get the Adjutant of the state to accept them as a company of the State Militia under the plea that there were already more companies in this district than the law designed, and such being the case, the State would not furnish them with uniforms and guns, so in the spring of 1882 the organization disbanded.

I noticed in the Lyndon Leader November 10, 1881 that Capt Finch and Lieut. C. P. Drew, of Co. I, 1st. Regt. Kansas State Militia, Burlingame, Kansas same down the previous Friday evening and administered the required oath to the Lyndon Guards. After which an election of officers was held by which J. H. Stavely was elected Capt., G. W. Morris 1st Lieut., and J. W. Bain 2nd Lieut. Then, November 29th, Jas. Bain having resigned to go away, a meeting was called to fill his office. Thereafter I found no further mention.

LIST OF MEMBERS

Columbian Camp, No. 126, Sons of Veterans.

—o—

NAME.	AGE '97.	BIRTHPLACE.	FATHER'S NAME.	FATHER'S REG'T.
W. A. Green.	33	Pennsylvania.	W. H. Green,	202 Pa. Inft.
E. C. Wilson,	21	Indiana.	A. L. Wilson,	84 Ind.
Thos. Sowell.		Kansas.	J. H. Sowell,	2 Colo. Cav.
Harry Rogers.	37	Illinois,	Wm. Rogers,	130 Ill. Vol.
L. T. Hussey,	31	Ohio,	Jerry Hussey,	34 Ohio.
Will Weber.	23	Kansas,	Geo. Weber,	11 Penn. Res.
Ed Swisher,	29	Illinois,	H. C. Swisher,	85 Ill.
J. I. Sweezey,	36	Indiana,	W. C. Sweezey,	140 Ind.
C. Hollingsworth,	26	Iowa,	N. Hollingsworth,	10 Ill.
John Evans,	22	Illinois,	J. Evans,	196 Ohio.
John Woods,		"	J. W. Woods,	15 Ill. Inft.
All Starr,	27	Kansas,	O. S. Starr,	3 Ohio Cav.
Geo. B. Weber,	35	Pennsylvania,	John Weber,	134 Pa.
E. A. Powell,			L. W. Powell,	116 Ohio.
Frank Downs,	29	Iowa,	F. Downs,	10 Iowa.
Fred Swisher,	23	Illinois,	H. C. Swisher,	85 Ill.
Lloyd Green,	26	Ohio.	W. D. Green,	192 Ohio.
C. Dougherty,	28	W. Virginia,	R. M. Dougherty,	15 W. Va. Inft.
Leslie Fix,		Kansas,	C. W. Fix,	9 Kan. Cav.
Ed Rockey.			J. S. Rockey,	105 Pa.
Will Starr,	23	Kansas,	O. S. Starr.	3 Ohio Cav.
W. H. Prather,	26	"	B. Prather,	24 Ind. Inft.
H. Woodward,	22	"	C. E. Woodward,	1st N. Y. Art.
W. H. Wynne,		Missouri,	R. H. Wynne,	1st Mo. S. M.
Rum Oard.		Indiana,	G. W. Oard,	83 Ind.
Ed McWhinney,	24	Illinois,	L. McWhinney,	123 Ill.
Wm. Plaunty,		Michigan,	J. Plaunty,	1st U. S. Eng.
W. D. Criley.	25	Ohio,	A. H. Criley,	44 Ohio.
Elza Rogers,	24	W. Virginia.	Jas. Rogers,	15 Va.
Will Rock,	39	Indiana,		5th Ind. Cav.
John Capper,	21	Sac and Fox A.,	A. Capper,	Gunboat U. S. N.
W. L. Kirkbride,	30	Ohio,	J. M. Kirkbride,	179 Ohio.
E. B. Kirkbride,	26	"	"	"
Chas. Bessee.	33	Illinois,	B. F. Bessee,	75 Ill. Inft.
I. P. Darnell,	23	Kansas,	A. J. Darnell,	2 Kan. Cav.
Frank Swisher.	21	Illinois.	H. C. Swisher,	85 Ill.
Will Ringhisen.	23	Kansas,	F. Ringhisen,	58 Ohio.
Mart Goodrich,	22	Ohio,	H. L. Goodrich,	145 N. Y.
Bart Hollingsworth,	21	Kansas,	N. Hollingsworth,	10 Ill. Inft.
J. S. Kittrell,	21	Tennessee,	J. M. Kittrell,	2nd Tenn.
W. F. Miller,	42	Indiana,	G. W. Miller,	21 Kan. S. M.

NAME.	AGE '97.	BIRTHPLACE.	FATHER'S NAME.	FATHER'S REG'T.
A. E. Madaris,	21	Kansas,	W. A. Madaris,	21 Kan. S. M.
W. H. Starkey,	21	"	John Starkey,	191 Ohio.
W. H. Shideler,	23	Indiana,	E. Shideler,	81 Ind. Inft.
Henry Oberfelt,	40	Missouri.	———————	- Mo. Inft.
C. M. Hinton,	23	Kansas,	James J. Hinton,	130 Ill. Inft.
Chas. Ringhisen,	26	"	F. Ringhisen,	58 Ohio.
J. F. Wilden.		Missouri,	Geo. Wilden,	40 Ill Inft.
E. Spurgin,	30	Tennesssee.	J. E. Spurgin.	Tenn Scout.

HISTORY OF THE SONS OF VETERANS.

Columbian Camp No. 126, Lyndon.

Long after the old soldiers had joined the Post and the Womans Relief Corps had been in active organization the old soldiers' boys got up interest enough to unite and form a camp. The old soldiers had to brace them up a good deal, perhaps because a majority of them were pretty young. They organized their camp here at Lyndon about September 1, 1893.

OFFICERS.

W. A. Green..................Capt.
E. C. Wilson..............1st Lieut,
Tom Sowell.............2nd Lieut,
Will Weber...............1st Sergt,
Ed Swisher.............Q. M. Sergt.

1894.

W. A. Green..................Capt.
George Weber............1st Lieut,
Frank Downs............2nd Lieut.
Will Weber..............1st Sergt,
Ed Swisher.............Q. M. Sergt.

1895.

Geo. Weber..................Capt,
Clint Hollingsworth.....1st Lieut,
I. P. Darnell.............2nd Lieut,
W. D. Criley..............1st Sergt,
Ed Swisher.............Q. M. Sergt.

After several meetings which were poorly attended, they died out for the balance of the year.

1896.

Two or three meetings in May were held and a reorganization was effected as follows:

W. A. Green..................Capt,
Ed Swisher..............1st Lieut,
I. P. Darnell.............2nd Lieut,
Will Weber...............1st Sergt,
W. D. Criley ....Q. M. Sergt.

There have been no further meetings held since So many of the Sons of Veterans belong to the Band and to other organizations that there does not seem to be room or time to carry the Sons of Veterans. The country boys, who desire it the most, are the poorest to keep up any regular attendance, and for the time being the order is slumbering, although they can and do turn out good firing squads on soldier funeral occasions, and Capt. Wilbur Green is ready to meet with the camp on all occasions.

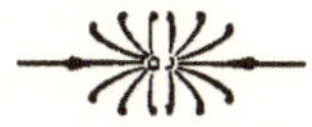

NELS HOLLINGSWORTH.

The Sixth Commander of Lyndon Post 1891.

His wife, Mrs. Martha Hollingsworth, at the same time being President of The Womans Relief Corps, No. 146.

Nelson Hollingsworth was born June 7, 1841 in Wayne county, Indiana. His parents removed from there to Oquaka, Henderson county, Ill. when he was five years old. There were six boys in the family who grew up, of which Nelson was next to the youngest. His father had a water grist mill in Oquaka on Fall creek, and also a farm. Nelson says that he put in most of his youth working around the mill, getting only a common school education.

He was twenty years old when the war commenced and early went as a volunteer.

In his language he says:

"I enlisted in Co. E, 10th Ill. Inft. in July, 1861. It was among the first three-years regiments raised. There were companies in it from all over the state, who, failing to go out in the three months service, still kept up organizations for drill purposes, and after the disastrous battle of Bull Run were ready at once to respond to President Lincoln's call for three-year men.

Our Captain was Charles Cowan, who had been our county clerk 12 years and was an elderly man having the esteem of all who knew him.

The company was slow in reporting; and was the last of the ten companies to join the regimental organization at Cairo August 28, 1861. We remained here until fall, when we moved to Mound City, Ill., opposite Kentucky. Thence, in February, we took a scout of two weeks into Kentucky, about the days when Genl. Grant was fighting at Fort Donelson. Soon after this we were put into the Mississippi Army that began the reduction of Island No. 10. We captured New Madrid. We were in Gen'l Pope's army on the Missouri side. This, Mar. 13, 1862, was our first engagement, and April 8th the rebels evacuated Island No 10.

After this we went down the Mississippi on transports scouting, but after Grant's troops fought the battle of Pittsburg Landing or Shiloh, Genl. Halleck called us back to help in the siege of Corinth. We went on transports up the Mississippi and Tennessee rivers. This siege of Corinth was a very tedious affair. Genl. Halleck had been appointed over Genl. Grant and had a large army but was afraid to attack the rebel army, and so every mile and half mile that he advanced upon the enemy at Corinth he had the army stop and build a long line of entrenchments. Corinth was 30 miles from Shiloh and took a month for Halleck to advance and lay siege to the enemy's real stronghold, only to lose the whole game; for Gen. Beauregard evacuated and went off on the cars before Old Halleck had scarcely fired a shot. After that he was called to Washington and Genls. Grant, Sherman, Rosecrans and others given a chance.

From here we were in the part of the army sent to garrison Nashville under Genl. Negley, where we remained from July, 1862 to June, 1863. We were on duty there during the battle of Stone River, and went out toward Murfreesboro, but only as support to Rosecran's army.

June 24, 1863 when the campaign for Chattanooga commenced, as Rosecran's army advanced and took possession of the country, our regiment garrisoned several places along the railroad leading to Chattanooga, Stevenson, the Sequatchee Valley, and up and down the Tennessee river, and wherever the line of communication was in danger of raids from rebel cavalry, there we tried to protect. We had no hand in the Chickamauga battle, but when Missionary Ridge was fought our whole regiment was sent with Genl. Sherman to the relief of Genl. Burnside and his besieged army at Knoxville. When we returned from that expedition, which we did immediately, we did garrison duty no longer, but went into the main army. We camped at Rossville, a few miles out from Chattanooga, and in December, 1863, our regiment having nearly all veteraned, we went home to Illinois on furlough. We went to Quincy as a regiment, leaving our guns and equipments there, and having one month's leave of absence. Those who did not re-enlist of our regiment, some 40 or 50, kept the camp and baggage wagons at Rossville, so that we returned there and took our place in Genl. Jeff C. Davis' division of the 14th corps.

When Genl. Sherman commenced the Atlanta campaign we were on hand and took a part in the first fighting of that 100-days battle. Our regiment was commanded by Col. John Tillson.

After the battle of Atlanta, July 22, when Genl. McPherson was killed, we were transferred to Genl. Mowers' division of the 17th Army Corps.

We marched with Sherman to the sea and had a hand in the taking of Savannah. When the campaign against the Carolinas commenced our corps was transferred by ocean transports up the coast to Beauford, South Carolina, and our operations with others in conjunction soon obliged the rebels to evacuate Charleston We had a hard fight at Bentonville; the rebels came down on us unexpectedly, in force, and our brigade in particular with fighting at front and rear both by day and night had all it could do until reinforced to save itself from capture.

Next afterwards we fought the rebels at Goldsboro, N. C., then we moved to Raleigh and soon after this we heard of Lee's surrender and President Lincoln's assassination. We were here when the rebel Genl. Johnson surrendered to Genl. Sherman. We marched to Washington, where we took part in the Grand Review. Then to Louisville, Ky. on the cars, where, July 4, 1865, we were mustered out of the U. S. service; then to Chicago where, July 12th, we got our discharges and pay.

I was a private all the way through, and saw about four years' service. I returned to Oquaka, Ill. This meant in Indian 'Yellow Banks,' and during the Black Hawk war was where Elisha Olcott, Sr. did service in an Illinois regiment for his country.

I stayed here a couple of years helping to run the grist mill for father.

I was married December 25, 1866 to Martha Titherington. In the spring of 1870 I moved to Cedar county, Iowa where I stayed two years, farming; then, having a brother, Enoch Hollingsworth, in Osage county, Kansas, I moved down there. He lived in Junction township. I landed there October 19, 1872 with my wife and three children. Not finding very much to do there, I went over to Peterton and engaged in the coal business. I lived near there and followed farming a little, and hauling coal to Lyndon for four years. Then I moved to Lyndon, buying a house and several lots over near Mrs. Varner's place. There I lived until April, 1884, when I built and moved to the west side of town where I have lived ever since.

Eight children have been born to us, seven of which are alive and five of which live at home.

Effie Jane Hollingsworth' the eldest, married Lee Smell, who abandoned her and since which time she and her child have lived at home with me.

Harry D. died, aged 4, at Peterton

John Clinton, who has recently married and set up for himself, lives here in Lyndon.

Edith May, who married Olla Fleming, lives here in Lyndon.

Barton Leslie, at home.

Rachel Vestal, at home.

Myrtle Ivey, at home.

Murray Blaine, the baby, age 13, at home.

——o——

THE LYNDON BANDS.

Of the original band formed in July or August, 1880, four members only seem to be left at Lyndon:—Hod Whitman, Will Olcott, Tony Richardson and Oll Deaver.

Hod Whitman had most of the papers and records of this organization in a drawer in their drug store and they were all burned up in the big fire of January 31, 1895, but by a month's searching among old papers and several talks with various members of the different bands in the 17 years that have elapsed since the history commenced, I glean the following, and if I am in error I desire to be corrected:

Nothing adds to patriotism more than good bands which are willing to turn out and play upon the occasions that draw our citizens together.

A great many individual musicians are found in places, who, having changed their abode, are lost from their organizations, but who, with their past experience and their horns are of great assistance in towns that regularly maintain a band. I cannot begin to tell the number of such persons who have played here with our Lyndon bands in the last 16 years; very often helping us all out of bad predicaments. I can say truly that this town has supported bands as faithfully as it has churches; $500 is a low estimate for the cost of the instruments, uniforms, wagon, year's instruction and other outlay before a good body of players can feel satisfied to go before the public and play on a big occasion. $50 or $75 taken in by festivals or stand privileges three or four times a year is the full extent of public help. The burden falls mainly on their own purses, and the many hours spent in practice would almost fit an individual for teaching.

I expect that the want of a band of their own in Lyndon was made manifest about July 6, 1880, when the Knights of Honor laid to rest the first member who died out of their organization, viz: Elias A. Barrett. The committee managing the funeral obsequies hired the Quenemo band of probably a dozen members, to come up and help.

Thereby hangs a tale: Mr. Barrett was laid to rest and long before the close of that summer day the Quenemo band went on their way home by C. R. Green's place down on the Quenemo road. At Henry Johnson's the boys found it necessary to stop and have a drink—of water. Having lately moved on from Ohio with a car load of traps, I had put in a few barrels of four year old cider to see if I couldn't work up a market here for my car load that I had left behind. I lived opposite Johnson's, and when they stopped, knowing the driver and desiring to transact some business, I went out to the wagon while the rest were in Henry's yard. At the close of my business I told Mr. Wilson, the driver, who was also a member of the band, that if the boys wished to sample my sour cider to invite them down, and I returned to the house. Directly, while I was at supper, hearing a noise of approaching footsteps I looked up the path and beheld the band in single file bearing down upon me. So I got a gallon measure and a glass and went to a barrel of my best cider vinegar and drew for them to drink. Knowing the one Wilson—although there were other Wilson brothers in the band about as numerous as the Swisher brothers in the present Lyndon Sons of Veterans Band—I handed it to him and he downed the tumbler full at about two gulps. Some of the others gagged upon tasting it, but not to be bluffed off with two dozen eyes watching them, downed theirs, and with the exception of Dr. Ashby, who was then a member, every last one took their whole tumbler full of sour cider. When it came to the second round Wilson took his by hard work; the rest declined.

The boys had left their horns up in the wagon, and not having to use much wind to get back to their conveyance, carried away straight faces, but I was told by some of them and others that they gagged and "heaved jonah" all the way home to Quenemo.

After that whenever they passed my place, be it night or day, I was always treated to a series of toots and cat wailings that let me know that they were still alive and holding "Vinegar Green's" treat in lively remembrance.

The joke thus unceremoniously perpetrated advertised my goods all over the country, so that afterwards when I drove up to a man's house to sell my stuff he could tell me at once whether they wanted it or not, and in two years I sold and traded away over one thousand dollars' worth of that shipment of Ohio cider vinegar.

Asking the reader's pardon for this long digression from Lyndon band history, I will go back to July, 1880.

Bob Miller, Hod Whitman, Tony Richardson, Will Olcott, Oll Deaver and a lot of others, consulting with the Lyndon merchants and prominent citizens, concluded that a band could be organized, and a subscription paper was passed around, the citizens giving $50 or $60. The band boys pledged the rest. W. C. Chatfield, leader of the Burlingame band, negotiated with Julius Bauer, Musical Instrument dealer of Chicago, for eleven instruments—brass horns and a snare drum, for which Lyndon paid $162.00. The services of Harry Dunn were procured for the first instructor. After a month or two Frank Holmes was hired as an instructor, followed by James W. Bain, all that fall of 1880.

The names of the members of the Band in 1880 were about as follows:

Tom Dempster,	Will Miller,
Rob. A. Miller,	E. D. Atwell,
Oll C. Deaver,	Horace Whitman,
H. H. Richardson,	Will S. Olcott.
Geo. Stanfield,	Will West,
Fred Jenness,	Ed Atwell, Jr.

Perhaps a few extracts from the Lyndon Leader of those days of 1880–'81–82 of which a member of the band was one of the proprietors, may give us a glimpse of past history in as condensed a form as any way.

"Christmas eve, 1880, the Lyndon Cornet Band attends the Presbyterian Church festivities and discourses sweet music."

January 1, 1881.—"The L. C. B. is making rapid advancement under the leadership of J. W. Bain." His services are reingaged about this time for another term.

Jan. 15th —"The band played on the streets in honor of the Knights of Honor the evening of the 10th when it was so cold that their instrument's froze up."

Feb. 5th.—"A citizen complains about the county sheriff, Harry Smith, shutting the band out of the court house, although Tom Dempster, a county deputy assures him that the coal is of his own furnishing."

February 12th number contains a piece of poetry written by the editor, Ed Vail, which is too good to languish in the old newspaper files "when the band blows."

OUR BOYS.

Who will say they're not proud of "our boys?"
Be they boys in blue or boys who blow,
But the "boys that blow" not the boys in blue,
Are the boys I wish to talk of, to you.

Now Lyndon could not boast, you know
Of a man or boy six months ago,
Who could pick up a horn and run the scale,
And run it correctly and never fail.

Now who can say they're not proud of "our boys?"
When in six months' time they have learned from a noise
To make music either loud or soft, and sweet to hear
As the gentle zephyr wafts it back to our ear.

Then stand firm by our "boys who blow,"
As you did by the boys in blue.
For our "boys who blow" have to battle you know,
As well as the boys in blue in that long long ago.

Our band it is an honor, our band it is all right.
So blow away boys, blow with all your might.
But don't lose courage or faint by the way,
For the Lord will provide you somewhere to play.

Three cheers for "our boys!" Hurrah for the right!
It will always conquer wrong, no matter how hard the fight.
So stand firm by "our boys," as firm as you can,
And say in one voice, we are proud of our band.

Mar. 12, '81—The L. C. B. held an entertainment in Prof. Whitman's new building, which was used several months thereafter for an opera house, until he got his stock of drugs. The band entertainment netted them $60.50. A contest was gotten up by which the prettiest lady present was to be awarded on vote a handsome pair of vases. Miss Lou Munger, of Carbondale, escorted thither by F. Bowman, was the successful contestant.

June 30, '81—The band elects their officers: Pres., E. D. Atwell; Vice Pres., G. L. Wales; Secy., R. A. Miller; Treas., H. S. Whitman; Leader, Jas. W. Bain.

This summer the Osage County Battalion is organized and as Col. H. K. McConnell and W. W. Morris, two of its chief promoters held office at the county seat, the L. C. B. becomes enthused with the military spirit in Lyndon and vote to attend the State Fair and Old Soldiers' Reunion at Topeka, September 15th. They buy themselves uniform caps, and after the doings at Topeka go to Lawrence and play for Gen. Weaver, the Greenback orator from Iowa. Also after their return home turning out to escort Weaver into Lyndon, where he spoke.

Thanksgiving time, 1881.—Will S. Olcott, who has just got home from his wedding tour and is a member of the band, gets a good serenade and in turn sets out a fine supper for the band. J. W. Bain, who for 13 months has been instructor of the band, having accepted a position down at Ossawatomie, resigns. He has been a good teacher and all regret his approaching departure.

NOTE BY AUTHOR.—He goes away only for a short time, when, not liking it, he returns and takes a cornet in the band again.

The Thansgiving festival netted the band $50.

January, '82, L. M. Roth, a dentist and a good musician, comes to Lyndon and in time joins the band.

May 18, '82 another band festival, $60.

June 22nd, the band boys beginning to buy new horns—better ones, made out of silver. H. H. Richardson buys a fine cornet; a fine snare drum bought.

June 23. They attend in a body the closing day school picnic down at the Knouff district, Miss Ella Gibson, teacher.

July 4, '82. Band goes to Reading, get $60 for their services, and all expenses.

Aug. 31—The L. C. B. and Osage City Martial bands furnish the music for the mass meeting in Lyndon when Senator P. B. Plumb addressed the old soldiers, and the Osage County Battalion held election of officers and arranged to go to Topeka.

Sept. 15th to 20th, the L. C. B. attends the Topeka Old Soldiers' Reunion with the Osage County Battalion, and the 16th enters the ring to contest for the 2nd musical prize, some six bands competing, which they failed to secure.

After the boys all got home the Burlingame paper of the 21st in commenting on the band playing at Topeka said that the Lyndon and Burlingame bands played among the best and that instead of the bands at Waterville and Williamsburg carrying away the first and second prizes respectively, it should have been the Burlingame and Lyndon bands.

The Lyndon paper of that time remarks that so many are gone away attending the doings at Topeka that the streets look deserted. The days prior to this had been ones of hot winds, the record reading, Sept. 12th, hot winds and dust; 13th, ditto; 14th, ditto, thermometer 114 in the shade. These hot winds cut the corn crop very short, the price being from 50 cents to 75 cents here, and 75 cents to $1 in St. Louis.

The fall of 1882, one time the band was out over to Osage City with four horses making a good show, when the Osage City photographer called them to halt and took their pictures just as they were in the wagon. Hod Whitman says that he has one of the pictures and the following persons show up in it: Tom Dempster, Lew Danhauer, Frank Whitman, Horace Whitman, Rob Miller, L. M. Roth, Jim Ayers, Fred Jenness and J. H. Smith.

I cannot follow the band thus closely any longer. July 4, 1883 Osage City had a big county celebration, among other things inviting the several bands of the county to play for a prize there, but when the L. C. B. desired to enter the contest the judges ruled them out because they had Jesse Cowan and James Smith in their ranks, who, the Osage City, folks claimed were members of other bands. Jesse Cowan had moved to Lyndon the fall of 1882. He had been a member of the Williamsburg band at the Topeka contest. These two players had taken the place of either two sick members or some who had moved away, and when the

Osage City folks objected, our band got so hot they offered to stake $100 upon their being the best players in the county, then and there putting up $25, and to have the contest come off in 30 days. But no one took them up.

Here is a list of our band members present on that occasion:

J. W. Bain................1st E b,
Jas. Smith................2nd E b,
H. H. Richardson..........1st B b,
Frank Whitman.............2nd B b,
L. M. Roth, leader........Alto B b,
Fred Jenness..............Solo alto,
Will West.................1st Alto,
R. A. Miller..............2nd Alto,
Geo. Miller...............1st Tenor,
Jesse Cowan...............2nd Tenor,
Lew Danhauer..............Baritone,
H. S. Whitman.............Tuba,
Ed Atwell.................Bass drum,
Ed Barrett................Tenor drum.

They were nicely uniformed, and I remember it was with feelings of pride that I saw them at this Osage City celebration. Lyndon turned out a great throng to accompany them there and join by invitation in the doings. We got treated miserably, all of us, and after that Lyndon and Osage City exchanged no more celebrations, and thereafter Lyndon planned good rousing celebrations at home and gave the band the benefit of the proceeds.

The band did not go up to Topeka that fall, for some reason.

Nov. 8, 1883, the band was called on to follow the remains of one of their members to the grave. Will West died on the 6th from the effects of being burned in an explosion of gasoline. This was the first death of any of their number, and there is always a sadness every decoration day as the band in each succeeding year has gathered around Will's grave to play their dirge. Now of late years Tom Dempster adds another grave to their list.

Some time at the beginning of 1884 the band reorganized and took the name of the Post, calling themselves the "Lyndon Post No. 19 G. A. R., Band."

There was a good deal going on this year of 1884—The Fourth, Decoration Day, Soldiers' Reunion at Leavenworth and late in the fall a county soldiers' reunion at Lyndon, the soldiers and the band all working in harmony.

Decoration Day, 1884, Harry Ford having that year set up a gallery in Lyndon, took 4 pictures. Two of the flower girls, one of the Post and one of the Band.

The band stood in a circle in front of Richardson's hotel, and the following members show in that picture:

F. H. Coney,	H. H. Richardson,
Frank Whitman,	Fred Jenness,
James H. Ayers,	Robt. A. Miller,
George Miller,	Jesse Cowan,
James H. Smith,	Horace Whitman,
Walter Kirby,	Tom Dempster,

Ed Barrett.

BALD HEAD BAND.

Space will admit of no further history. The band went down by removals, but the members remaining here have always managed to get out a band, small or great, for Decoration days and the band at present in Lyndon under the leadership of M. L. Laybourn, known as the "Bald-Head Band," is nothing more than a continuation of the old Lyndon Post Band of 1884, with some old and some new members.

They were organized about May 1, 1896, about as follows:

H. S. Whitman,	W. S. Olcott,
H. H. Richardson,	C. S. Alexander,
W. A. Greene,	J. M. Cowan,

J. H. Buckman,	L. T. Hussey,
Wm. Rock,	Dick Miles,
J. H. Newell,	R. C. Buckman,
Kit Wilson,	Floyd Pleasant,

M. L. Laybourn, Leader.

—

THE SONS OF VETERANS BAND.

The want of a good strong band among the young men was made manifest in the summer of 1894, and not desiring to reorganize any old band, but to build up a new one entirely, a party of young men organized August 9, '94, and hired M. L. Laybourn for their instructor for one year.

Decoration Day, 1895 the Sons of Veterans Band, as they styled themselves, acquitted themselves so well that the old soldiers went to them and offered to help get up a big "Fourth of July," and let the band furnish the program and have all the receipts from sale of stand rights, etc. The day came, and everything was carried out to perfection until about 3 p. m., when a sudden rain storm came up and dispersed the crowd, but as it was, quite a snug sum was realized to help along the band expenses.

August 9, '95 the band found it not best to longer hire Mr. Laybourn's services as instructor, and since that time they have got along very well under the leadership of Sam'l J. Jones, and when out on public occasions make as good a showing as ever any band has here in Lyndon.

The following names are about a correct list of those who were in the band July 4, 1895:

J. D. Swisher,	Charles Daugherty,
E. A. "	Wm. Rock,
F. C. "	L. T. Hussey,
F. T. "	W. A. Greene,
B. H. "	Clint Hillingsworth
John Capper,	Bart "
Dewey Gardner,	O. A. Fleming,
Chas. Wilson,	Roy Wright,
Gene "	Stewart Gill,

Milt Rogers.

There have been several who were in the band a short time whose names I have not been able to get. Upon request the present leader of the band, S. J. Jones, gave me a list of the members as they were New Years day, 1897.

List of the present members of the Sons of Veterans Band, Lyndon:

Stewart Gill................Picalo,
Roy Wright................Picalo,
A. B. Thurman........E b Cornet,
Fred Swisher......Solo B b Cornet,
S. J. Jones........Solo B b Cornet,
Bert Swisher..............1st B b,
John Widney ....2nd B b,
Chas. Wilson...........Solo Alto,
Ollie Fleming.............1st Alto,
Millard Rogers...........2nd Alto,
Eugene Wilson...Slide Trombone,
A. H. Gardner..........1st Tenor,
Clint Hollingsworth....2dd Tenor,
H. P. Corothers.........3rd Tenor,
Frank Swisher...........Baritone,
Chas. Dougherty......1st Eb Bass,
Ed Swisher..........2nd Eb Bass,
Sigel Gill.............Snare Drum,
Bart Hollingsworth...Bass Drum.

Officers of the S. of V. Band.

Board of directors, Charles Wilson, Fred Swisher and Clint Hollingsworth; President, A. H. Gardner; Secretary, Frank Swisher; Treasurer, Bart Hollingsworth; Leader, S. J. Jones.

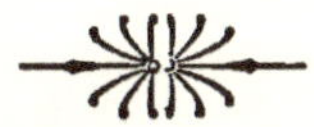

JOEL H. BUCKMAN.

8th Commander of Lyndon Post No. 19.

Joel H. Buckman was born October 1, 1844 in Sangamon county, Ill. At the age of 6 his parents moved to Tazwell county, where their home was ever after. Joel was the oldest in a family of eight children, seven of which are alive to-day. He lived and worked at home on a farm near Green Valley until he enlisted. He only had such educational advantages as the common district schools of those early days afforded, and was just about going away to school when Lincoln's call for 300,000 volunteers in July, 1862 was sounded over the northern land.

The 71st, 72nd and 73rd Illinois were early organized, and in the race as to which should first be ready for the mustering officer, the 73rd was ahead.

J. H. Buckman enlisted July 21, '62 at Delavan, Ill., in Capt. Wilder B. M. Colts' company—Co. B, 73rd Ill., and gathered immediately at Camp Butler near Springfield, where their regiment was organized, and August 21, '62 mustered into the U. S. service, the 71st and 72nd coming in behind them one or two days.

The 73rd was known as the "preacher regiment," a good many preachers being both officers and members; and only March 4, 1897 I saw a mention of the death of Capt. Peter Wallace, age 84, at Chicago, member of the 73rd Ill., the "preacher regiment."

Within a week of their muster into the service they left for Dixie—August 27th—landing at Louisville, Ky., where they stayed until Sept. 11th, when the rebel Genl. Kirby Smith made his raid toward Cincinnati, O, they were immediately sent to Covington to assist in the defense. After the danger was over here, the regiment with many others was hurried back, Sept. 28th, to Louisville, and went right on to Muldraugh's Hill to head off the rebel Gen. Bragg and help the old troops get into Louisville. In the race northward the rebels would have captured Louisville had it not been for the new levies rallying promptly to its rescue.

Here at Louisville their regiment was assigned to Col. F. Schaeffer's Brigade, Genl. Phil. H. Sheridan's Division, Gilbert's Corps, but later on commanded by Alex McCook.

October 1st, his 18th birthday, they marched out to meet the rebels in battle but did not corner Old Bragg until the 8th, when at Perryville the 73rd Ill. got into the engagement good and strong, and received its first baptism in blood.

From there they marched and countermarched with Rosecran's army on down to Edgefield Junction, where the Division stopped, Nov. 7th, while most of the army went on beyond Nashville and camped.

When the railroad and tunnel at Gallatin were repaired, Sheridan moved his division to Camp Mill Creek, 7 miles southeast of Nashville in readiness for Rosecrans' advance to give battle at Murfreesboro. But here we have to stop and follow Comrade Buckman's story another way, for measles claimed him now from his command, and Hospital No. 14, Nashville and Sheridan's convalescent camp two or three miles from the city, was his home several months. After measles came the dreaded army disease, chronic diarrhœa, which so reduced him that he was given a discharge May 4, 1863. But unable to travel alone, he would have died right there at Nashville, had not his father, Mr. C. F. Buckman, come on from Illinois and helped him home.

He remained at home until Sept., '64, when he re-enlisted in his old Co. B, 73rd Ill, and joined them at Nashville. The regiment had all this time been in the main army under Sheridan in Genl. Schaeffer's Brigade of the 20th Corps.

October 20, 1863, after the battle of Chickamauga, in the reorganization of the Cumberland Army, Newton commanded the Div. and Steadman the Brigade, but when Buckman joined his regiment at Nashville Genl. Opdycke commanded the 1st Brig. and Genl. W. L. Elliott the Division, being the 2nd of the 4th Corps, Genl. T. J. Wood being the Corps commander to the end of the war.

The regiment had gone through all the battles and needed recruits bad enough. Buckman had been in their ranks before, but there were lots of others who had not, and the battle of Nashville gave them all a chance to distinguish themselves. This was Dec. 15th and 16th, and at its close the union troops pursued the defeated rebels down to the Harpeth Shoals on the Tennessee river, where Hood escaped to the south, and Buckman's Division encamped at the beautiful city of Huntsville, along with other parts of Genl. Thomas' army. Early in February most of the 4th corps were transported on the cars up into East Tennessee, above Knoxville, where they were ready to head Genl. Lee off if he should attempt to flee that way from Richmond. Here the end of the war found them.

The total number of men, including officers and recruits, mustered in the 73rd Regt. of Ill. Vol. Inft. from the beginning to the end of its service, was 972.

At the close of the war the regiment found that during their three years' serv.ce they had lost as follows:

Total killed on battlefield	53
Total died of wounds	45
Total died of disease	102
Total died in prison, starvation etc,	16
Discharged before end of war by reason of wounds	36
Discharged before end of war by reason of disability	146
Transferred and promoted to other branches of service	129
Resigned service	29
Dismissed	1
Dishonoraby discharged	1
Deserted,	31
Unaccounted for	6
Missing and supposed killed	4
Mustered out at close of war	373
Total	972

The muster out at Nashville in May and discharge of the 73rd Ill. Inft., June 3, 1865 at Camp Butler, Ill, made J. H. Buckman a free man once more and not yet 21 years old.

He farmed there in Illinois at home until March, 1870, when he came to Burlingame, Kansas and accepted a position as clerk in Wm. Smith's store.

Oct. 9, 1872 he was married to Lida R. Richardson, at Burlingame. In 1874 he went back with his wife to Illinois on a visit, but settled down there and remained until 1885, when he returned to Kansas, settling down at Lyndon, where he has lived ever since. He was elected to the office of county clerk in 1889, filling it the term of 1890-91, but a change in the politics of many of his friends in 1892 caused the office to go to the Populist party afterwards.

Mr. Buckman has one child, Roy C. Buckman, born October 4, 1880.

Comrade Buckman has always been

a well posted man in the G. A. R. ritual and has frequently filled offices in the Grand Army.

Being a good singer, his services have always been in demand in the Glee Clubs of Lyndon on all times and occasions. Ever since his advent here he has been active in the Presbyterian church work, and acted as the superintendent of the Sunday school about ten years at one stretch.

With this brief synopsis of Comrade Buckman's life history, the historian leaves him to future historians to write up more fully.

——:——

A PICTURE

Of Historic Interest to the People of Lyndon.

Some of the G. A. R. boys of 1884.

——

Several months after Harry Ford first established his photograph gallery in Lyndon, on Decoration Day, 1884 he took several pictures out doors of various gatherings. The one I propose to speak about now is a picture of about 33 old soldiers belonging to the Post, taken in front of the post office, then in the west end of Lew Sargeant's old bank building, the site of which is now occupied by the Journal Block. Here all who happened to be present, which was not half the old soldiers of Lyndon, fell into line, firing squad to the right, and with a background of the Richadson Hotel, the Averill Hall and Steele's harness shop to shoot against, Harry Ford got a splendid picture of at least 28 faces.

Dr. E. B. Fenn and I being tall, got put over behind, so that only the upper part of the Doctor's face shows in the picture. In the foreground John H. Howe, D. H. Hanhauer, Josiah R. Drew, Fred Downs and Oscar Keenan, being officers of the post that year, and in front took splendid pictures. Wm. Haas held the colors. The firing squad, consisting of John M. Barnes, Clark E. Henderson, James Wells, Elijah Williams, John Lefler, John Hooper and George Thomas in the front rank and Amos Morris, S. L. McWhinney, Archibald Neff, N. Y. Buck, Basel Albaugh, George McMillen and Phillip Lefler all show up well. Grouped at the left of the colors were R. R. Glass, Fred Super, Patrick Daugherty Elijah Hedges, Dr. E. B. Fenn, Milton Whinrey, Dr. R. H. Chittenden, C. R. Green, David F. Coon, Daniel Dodge, a visiting comrade from over on the Dragoon and squarely behind Fred Downs stood Abel Primmer, known only by we who have preserved the tradition. Two or three others were also screened from a good view, so that no one now knows who they were. Several of the bystanders' faces in the rear show up good notably W. P. Bailey.

Thirteen years have elapsed. Of the 30 whose faces or forms we know in that picture, eleven only are present here; five are dead, 14 have removed, ten of them to other states.

In looking over the roll of the Post members of two years later—1886, I see that out of a membership then of 88 in good standing in the G. A. R., to-day, only eleven years later, only 40 remain in the vicinity of Lyndon, one half, or possibly a few over half being now members of the G. A. R. Sixteen have removed to other states, 20 to other places in Kansas, and 12, so far as we know, of that number are dead.

Their average age then was 47 years, Silas Tower being 70 and Tom Dempster 35. Adding ten years to their ages then would make an estimated average age now of old soldiers of 57 years.

C. R. Green.

THE TRIALS OF AN ARMY RECRUIT.

Who would not be a Soldier Boy,
To seek adventures like Rob Roy!
And as o'er countries I would roam,
I'd never think of going back home.
Refrain.
A soldier's life for me,
So glorious and so free.

Thus mused a farmer's boy one day
As by himself he turned the hay;
And he thought if he was only in some battle
How he would make his musket rattle.
A soldier boy I would be
So happy and so free.

Away to the war I'll strike a bee line,
And on the rolls my name I'll sign.
My old clothes I'll give to you
And in their place don soldier blue.
For a soldier I'm bound to be,
So to all, a good bye for me.

In my soldier suit how nice I can march.
It is no citizen's suit stiff with starch.
No more my feet shall I abuse,
Said he as he put on the army shoes.
A soldier boy, O write to me!
Now Old Dixie I'm bound to see.

Away down south in Dixie Land
He found there his own chosen band,
And as he took his place in the ranks
He thought not of old soldiers' pranks.
For a soldier he was going to be.
And the rebels he was going to see.

As he had been riding many a day
Soon on his blanket he slumbered away;
And so very sound was his sleep
That the boys stole his blanket from under his feet.
A soldier boy was he,
And old soldiers tricks didn't see.

For roll call, loudly the drums did beat,
And wildly our soldier started from his sleep.
The Rebs! The Rebs! Give me a gun!
And I'll go out and make them run,
A brave soldier I want to be,
So the first Reb, show him to me.

It is only roll call the sergeant replied.
As turning round the boys' fun he did chide.
Go back to bed and remember that the drum and fife
Help old soldiers to enjoy camp life.
A wise soldier you will never be
If old soldiers tricks you don't see.

It was here he first saw a hard-tack,
And many a one did he try to crack.
And his canteen had such a queer spout
It bothered him to make the water run out.

Then that haversack hung by his side,
With such rations to delight a soldier's pride;
And his great big knap-sack—
Which to carry almost broke his back.

His cartridge box and straps seemed so heavy,
As 'round they girted him for battle ready;
And with that heavy musket on his arm
He almost felt sorry he had ever left the farm.
Thus our new recruit, you see,
Was learning fast a soldier to be.

He also experienced that delightful sensation
That happens to soldiers in every station.
As over him the greybacks began to crawl
He much preferred to face the enemy's ball.

You'd have laughed to see him warm afternoons
Out scanning his shirt and pantaloons
But he learned soon that boiling in the camp kettle
His clothes, soon the lice and nits would settle.
It almost makes me blush gentlemen
To think of what we endured then.

The many weary days of fatigue work and drill,
It seems as if a recruit's patriotism it would kill.
But life in the "Sunny South" on the picket line
Or writing home from camp all beguiled away the time.

One day orders were quickly issued to the camp
For all able-bodied soldiers to get

ready for a tramp.
And our recruit buckled on his armour
for a fight;
Was it fear made him tremble when
out of sight?

A few miles they marched double-quick
Then formed in batt e line along a
creek;
And as the shells and bullets did rattle,
Began the new recruit's first battle.

Our recruit turned out to be a brave
lad,
And beside the old soldiers did n't
act bad.
Soon the boys welcomed him into their
mess,
For he's an old soldier along with the
rest.

——o——

DAVID F. COON,

Eleventh Commander of Lyndon Post.

D. F. Coon was born January 3, 1847 in Allen county, Ohio. He was raised there and was too young to go into the war at first, being only 14 years old when it commenced.

He enlisted February 29, 1864 as a recruit in the old 78th Ohio Vol. Infť., which had gone out to the war.

He joined his regiment at Chattanooga about a month later, in time to get some knowledge of military tactics before Genl. Sherman started out on his Atlanta campaign, May 4, 1864.

D. F. Coon belonged to the 3rd Brigade, 1st Division, 14th Army Corps.

Comrade Coon was is all that 100-days' battling that was carried on by Sherman's army on that campaign.

If any one wants to know more let him take up some one of the complete war histories and read the details. The history of one regiment one week was in a great measure the history of another regiment the next week. Sooner or later all would have similar experiences.

After the taking of Atlanta Comrade Coon was in that part of the army that marched with Sherman "down to the sea." Part of the time at the front helping to build roads or engaged in skirmishes; then again in the rear helping the wagon trains along.

After the taking of Savannah they soon started out on the campaign of the Carolinas and he had a hand in the Bentonville, Goldsboro and Raleigh engagements. They were at Raleigh when news of Lee's surrender came.

In due time Johnson surrendered to Sherman, and the army started on that racing march to see which should get to Washington first. They went via Richmond and up across the battlefields of the Potomac army. After taking part in the grand review they were transferred to Louisville where they were mustered out; then back to camp near Dayton, Ohio, where they were discharged July 15, 1865, and Mr. Coon returned home to Albany, Ohio. As he was yet only a young man of 18 he put in the next three years getting a better education there in Ohio. Then May, 1869 he came to Baldwin, Kansas and attended the Baker University. His folks had moved to the northern part of Osage county in 1866, so that Kansas became Comrade Coon's home. The next several years—eight at least—after D. F. Coon's advent in Kansas was spent by him in teaching school in two or three different counties, taking in the meanwhile a term or two at the state normal at Emporia. Finally in 1877 he ran for county office, and was elected surveyor.

His mother having died in 1878, he bought his father's property and became a real estate owner of the county where he has resided ever since, holding the office of county surveyor by appointment or election several times, which office he fills now.

WILLIAM RAND,

12th Commander of Lyndon Post—1897.

Born March, 1837, Bloomfield, Jefferson county, Ohio.

I learned the carpenter trade when 18. I followed that 25 years before and after the war. I commenced for myself when 21 years old.

June 6, 1858 I married Orinda L. Chapman, of Letartsville, Meigs county, Ohio, and made my home there 28 years. We had two boys born to us before I went to the war. Harvey L. Rand, who resides here in Lyndon, and is engaged in business with me, and Charles M. Rand, dealer in stock at Kansas City, Missouri.

I enlisted May 2, 1863 in Co. C, 140 O. V. I. I went at once into barracks at Gallipolis, Ohio, where we staid a week and then were sent to Charleston, W. Va.

Gallipolis is on the Ohio river opposite the mouth of the Kanawha river, and Charleston was perhaps 50 miles up the river, and a large portion of West Virginia west of the Alleghany mountains, and quite a portion of Virginia west of the Blue Ridge mountains was drained by the Kanawha river and its tributaries, such as the Gauley, Greenbrier, Bluestone, Little and New rivers. The latter taking head in North Carolina. All along these rivers between these two large ranges of mountains are smaller ranges and innumerable valleys settled with people, and before the war scarcely any railroads, so that as the union army penetrated these back regions in the mountains their supplies had to be drawn in wagons to them over rough roads, along mountainous streams where the rebel bushwhackers could dash in without warning and do their work and be off again before the officer at the head of the train could stop them.

This was the sort of a country that our 140th Ohio Inft. had to do their service in that season of 1863. Long marches of hundreds of miles up into these mountainous valleys, guarding trains of supplies to some of Genl. Crook's army at Meadow Bluffs, when every trip some one or more of our comrades in the company or regiment would be shot down from ambush by guerrillas. Little Sewell, Big Sewell and Floyd mountains are familiar land marks to us.

At first we camped near Charleston, W. Va., at Camp White, taking turns in scouting and guarding trains.

Our Colonel, Robert Wilson, was a man held in high regard by his boys.

Later in the season we moved to camp at Meadow Bluffs in Greenbrier county, among the mountains, and had to draw supplies 200 miles. There were perhaps 3,000 to 5,000 of us and opposed to us were the rebel Generals Jenkins and old Ex-Gov. Henry A. Wise. We had to work in conjunction with the union army over in the Shenandoah Valley opposing the rebel Genl. Early.

Soon after entering the service a skirmish had taken place, of two or three days' duration, at Fayetteville, about May 18th to 20th.

Sometimes the rebel army would number 2,500 to 4,000 in West Va, and then again they crossed over the Alleghany range into the Shenandoah Valley, and we would have only bushwhackers to fight, and our regiment would be scattered by companies for a hundred miles.

I do not know our losses by means of the bushwhackers. I do know that our regiment would much rather have been in one of the grand armies under

Rosecrans or Sheridan. But we filled the place assigned us, and did our duty and when our time was up went back to Gallipolis, Ohio and were mustered out of the U. S. service, Sept. 3, 1863.

I returned to Letartsville and went to work at my trade again.

I moved to Eskridge, Kansas, May 20, 1882. I followed carpentry two years; then bought a farm and went into the stock business with my boys.

We had two girls born to us in Ohio after the war: Mamie O. Rand in '66 and Daisy W. Rand in '77. Both are living.

Mamie is a stenographer with the Kansas Loan and Trust Co., of Topeka, where she has been for five years.

Daisy is studying music in Kansas City. Her home is here.

My wife Orinda died March 31, 1886 at Eskridge by reason of a lamp explosion which covered her with burning oil, and though I was near by and managed to smother the flames, it was not until she had received such injuries that she died some days later. The following October I was married to Mrs. Lorinda C. Buchanan, of Athens, Ohio. My wife had adopted a child there in Ohio—Miss Mabel—who became as one of our own children and has always lived with us.

February 13, 1895 I engaged in the lumber business at Lyndon, eventually buying the lumber yard and moving my family here and buying other Lyndon property and settling down as one of her citizens. WM. RAND.

NAMES

OF OLD SOLDIERS AND SAILORS Whose Graves are Decorated in the Lyndon Cemetery.

—

WEST SIDE.

James H. Rynerson, Kans.,	Lot No. 342
S. R. Shoemaker, Illinois,	" " 313
Wm. Gibson, Iowa,	" " 255
John Pettigrew, Illinois,	" " 257
J. H. Crowe, Indiana,	" " 201
E. A. Barrett, Kan. Militia,	" " 94
Geo. W. Herold, N. H.,	" " 17

....

....

....

....

....

....

....

....

—:—

EAST SIDE.

Geo. W. Oard, Indiana,	N. ½	Lot No. 61
E. B. Fenn, Iowa,	S. ½	" " 61
A. W. Newton, Ohio,	S. ½	" " 97
Frank Slouiker, Ind.,	N. ½	" " 210
Phillip Wingate, Indiana,		" " 217
Wallace Green, Indiana,		" " 230
Robt. J. Wynne, Kansas,		" " 258
Delas Watson, Kan. Militia,		" " 260

....

....

....

....

....

....

IN THE CIRCLE.

Elisha Olcott, Illinois,	Lot No. 579
Fred S. Sauers, Ohio,	" " 585
Francis A. Courtney, Ill.,	" " 590
John Courtney, W. Va.,	" " 590
J. Wm. Brooks, Illinois,	" " 595
T. E. Dempster, Navy,	" " 594
Simon Siples, Ohio,	" " 614
Patrick Daugherty, Mo.	" " 615
Martin Bannon, Ohio,	" " 603
Robert S. Fleming, Illinois.	" " 636
Geo. W. Pryer, Illinois,	" " 711
Fred S. Singletary, Tenn.,	" " 712
D. H. Danhauer, Ohio,	" " 686
Abram Primmer, Ohio,	" " 687

....

....

....

....

....

....

....

—:—

ON G. A. R. LOT BELOW THE CIRCLE.

Lewis A. Reynolds, Mich., Lot No. 450

....

....

....

....

—:—

Any one examining this list and desiring to know more about the history and death of these comrades. will find it under their respective states, pages 102 to 111 of the Soldiers Roster and History.

Abel Primmer died after that part of the Roster was printed. He was in the 33rd O. V. I. at the end of the war, and removed to Kansas about 1878. He died February 28, 1897. His widow and two or three children live here, Mrs. Munroe Stivison being one.

In the Dane cemetery in this township is buried Geo. Wesley Riggs, of 33rd Ill. Inft. who died May 20, 1882. His son, Lewis Riggs, lives near there with Andrew Peterson.

—:—

ADVERTISEMENT—ANNALS OF LYNDON.

——:-o-:——

THE 60 pages of this pamphlet are drawn from a book—"Annals of Lyndon"—that I have been working on for two years. A portion of it is printed, and I am working on it all the time, hoping that I may complete it in another year. 22 chapters of it were printed by the Current Remark during 1896.

Only a small edition, 200 copies more or less, will be printed. It is to be a book of 400 octavo, double column pages, just like this pamphlet. It will be bound in cloth and sold on subscription.

I have a vast amount of material, which I have been years in gathering, that enables me to give the early history of Lyndon and vicinity.

I have taken down the narratives of many old settlers, far and near, who have been instrumental in the making of the country adjacent to Lyndon.

I expect to interview many more of the old settlers.

The book will contain the history of everything that went to make up the city that had such a struggle to become the county seat of Osage county, and the pleasant home town with its railroads, its several schools, its six churches, its numerous orders and lodges, its old soldiers, its bands, and whatever is worthy of mention.

To the settlers for miles in every direction around Lyndon, who through 25 years have helped in her development, Lyndon is indebted, and mention will be made of every one so connected.

A list of the county officers from the beginning; lists of early settlers; the militia rolls; lists of present inhabitants, and many other things will be prominent features of this work—"Annals of Lyndon." C. R. GREEN.

——:—O—:——

www.ingramcontent.com/pod-product-compliance
Lightning Source LLC
Chambersburg PA
CBHW030719110426
42739CB00030B/850

* 9 7 8 3 3 3 7 3 0 6 6 9 4 *